Mistero Buffo
The Comic Mysteries

Some forty million people throughout the world have watched Dario Fo perform this brilliant one-man show. Displaying the same subversive wit of his notorious West End hits, *Accidental Death of an Anarchist* and *Can't Pay? Won't Pay!*, these 'Comic Mysteries' recreate the irreverent vitality of the popular medieval theatre.

Essential to an understanding of the well-springs of Fo's remarkable genius, *Mistero Buffo* appears here for the first time in English, with an informative introduction by Stuart Hood, editor of the Methuen edition of Fo's work.

'Based on careful research into the work of the strolling players of medieval Italy, the short excursions into different characters are memorable and hilarious.'

Ned Chaillet, *Wall Street Journal*

DARIO FO was born in 1926 in Lombardy. He began working in the theatre in 1951 as a comic and mime. Together with his wife, Franca Rame, he was highly successful as actor, director and writer of satirical comedies for the conventional theatre. In the Sixties they abandoned it; Fo began to write for a wider audience in factories and workers' clubs and produced work which was not only an important political intervention in Italy but has been internationally acclaimed. In 1970 he and his wife founded the theatrical collective, La Comune, in Milan. His work – and the work of Franca Rame – has been performed in England with great success: *Can't Pay? Won't Pay!* (Half Moon Theatre and Criterion Theatre, London, 1981); *Accidental Death of an Anarchist* (Half Moon Theatre and Wyndham's Theatre, London, 1980); *Female Parts* by Franca Rame (National Theatre, London, 1981); *Mistero Buffo* (Riverside Theatre, London, 1983); *Trumpets and Raspberries* (Palace Theatre, Watford; Phoenix Theatre, London, 1984); *Archangels Don't Play Pinball* (Bristol Old Vic, 1986) and *Elizabeth* (Half Moon Theatre, London, 1986).

Also by Dario Fo

Accidental Death of an Anarchist
Archangels Don't Play Pinball
Can't Pay? Won't Pay!
Elizabeth
Female Parts (co-author: Franca Rame)
Trumpets and Raspberries

Series editor: Stuart Hood

The front cover shows Dario Fo performing the Lazzo of the Fly *in* Zanni's Grammelot *from* Mistero Buffo. *(Copyright: La Comune). The photograph of Dario Fo on the back cover was taken by Max Whitaker.*

DARIO FO

Mistero Buffo
Comic Mysteries

Translated by ED EMERY
Edited and introduced by STUART HOOD

A Methuen Paperback

A METHUEN MODERN PLAY

This translation first published in 1988 by
Methuen London Ltd.,
11 New Fetter Lane, London EC4P 4EE.

Mistero Buffo copyright © 1969 by Dario Fo
Translation copyright © 1988 Ed Emery
Introduction copyright © 1988 Stuart Hood

Set in 10 on 11 Times Roman by Theatretexts,
Waterguard House, 1 Branch Road, London E14.
Printed in Great Britain by Richard Clay Ltd, Bungay,
Suffolk.

British Library Cataloguing in Publication Data

Fo, Dario
    [Mistero Buffo. *English*]. Mistero Buffo;
    The comic mysteries. —— (A Methuen modern play).
    I. Title II. Hood, Stuart
    852′.914   PQ4866.02
    ISBN 0-413-18380-7

CAUTION

Contents

INTRODUCTION
The Theatre of Dario Fo and Franca Rame

The son of a railway worker, Dario Fo was born in 1926 near
the Lago Maggiore in Northern Italy. He grew up in a village
community that included glass-blowers and smugglers, where
there was a strong tradition of popular narrative – much of it
humorously subversive of authority – fed by travelling
story-tellers and puppeteers. Gifted artistically, he studied
architecture at Milan at the art-school attached to the Brera
Gallery; but the theatre drew him strongly – first as a
set-designer and then as a performer. His career began in
revue which was the spectacular escapist entertainment of
post-war Italy with girls and comics (some very brilliant like
Totò, whom Fo greatly admired) and glamorous *chanteuses*.
It was a genre favoured by politicians of the ruling Christian
Democrat party; girls' legs were preferable to the social
preoccupations of contemporary Italian cinema. In revue Fo
began to make his mark as an extraordinarily original comic
and mime. On radio he built a reputation with his monologues
as a Poer Nano – the poor simpleton who, in telling Bible
stories, for example, gets things wrong, preferring Cain to the
insufferable prig, Abel. In 1954 he married Franca Rame, a
striking and talented actress, who came from a family of
travelling players and had made her first stage appearance
when she was eight days old. Together they embarked on a
highly successful series of productions.

In the fifties the right-wing clerical Christian Democrat
government had imposed a tight censorship on film, theatre
and broadcasting. Fo took advantage of a slight relaxation in

censorship to mount an 'anti-revue', *Il dito nell'occhio* (One in the Eye). His aim was clear – to attack those myths in Italian life which, as he said, 'Fascism had imposed and Christian Democracy had preserved.' *Il dito nell'occhio* was 'one in the eye' for official versions of history. Presented at the Piccolo Teatro in Milan it was an immense success to which the participation of the great French mime, Jacques Lecoq, from whom Fo learned much, was an important contribution. *Il dito nell'occhio* was the first in a series of pieces which drew on French farce, on the traditional sketches of the Rame family, and on the traditions of the circus. This mixture of spectacle, mime and social comment was highly successful but made the authorities nervous; the police were frequently present at performances, following the scripts with pocket torches to ensure that there were no departures from the officially approved text. Fo grew in stature and virtuosity as actor and comic, exploiting his extraordinary range of gesture, movement and facial expression, his variety of voices and accents, and his skill as a story-teller. It was the misfortune of Italian cinema that it was unable to exploit his talents. There were difficulties in finding suitable scripts and, on set, his vitality and spontaneity were denied the space and freedom that the theatre provided. But what Fo did take away from film was an understanding of how montage gave pace to narrative.

In 1959 the Dario Fo–Franca Rame company was invited to open a season at the Odeon Theatre in Milan. The piece they chose was *Gli arcangeli non giocano a flipper* (Archangels Don't Play Pinball), written, directed and designed by Fo. It was unusual in that it dealt critically with certain ludicrous aspects of Italian society. The middle-class audience were astonished by its rhythms and technique and delighted by Fo in the leading role – that of a wise simpleton, who looks back to Poer Nano and forward to a scries of similar clowns in later work. Fo and Rame were now securely established both as actors and as personalities in the public eye. Their success in conventional theatre was confirmed by a series of pieces which exploited a mixture of comedy, music and farcical plots in which Fo would, for instance, double as

an absent-minded priest and a bandit. The social references
were there – Fo and Rame were now both close to the
Communist Party and acutely aware of the political tensions
in society – and the public readily picked them up. In a period
which saw widespread industrial unrest culminating in the
general strike of 1960 their material caused the authorities in
Milan to threaten to ban performances.

Italian television had been for many years a fief of the
Christian Democrats. Programme control was strict: a young
woman given to wearing tight sweaters who looked like
winning a popular quiz show had to be eliminated on moral
grounds. But when in 1962 the centre-left of the Christian
Democrats became dominant there was some relaxation of
censorship. It was in these circumstances that the Fo–Rame
team was invited to appear on the most popular TV show,
Canzonissima, which, as its name suggests, featured
heart-throb singers along with variety acts. Into this show the
Fo's proceeded to inject their own brand of subversive
humour – such as a sketch in which a worker whose aunt has
fallen into a mincing-machine, which cannot be stopped for
that would interrupt production, piously takes her home as
tinned meat. The reaction of the political authorities and of
the right-wing press was to call for censorship, duly imposed
by the obedient functionaries of Italian television – all of them
political appointees. There was a tussle of wills at the end of
which the Fo's walked out of the show. The scandal was
immense. There were parliamentary questions; threats of
law-suits on both sides. Fo had public opinion solidly behind
him. He had, he said, tried to look behind the facade of the
'economic miracle', to question the view that 'we were all one
big family now' and to show how exploitation had increased
and scandals flourished. By subverting *Canzonissima* from
within he had established himself with a huge popular
audience.

During this period Fo had become interested in material
set in or drawn from the Middle Ages. He had begun 'to look
at the present with the instruments of history and culture in
order to judge it better'. He invited the public to use these
instruments by writing an ambitious piece, *Isabella, tre*

caravelle e un cacciaballe (Isabella, Three Caravels and a Wild-Goose Chaser), in which Columbus – that schoolbook hero – is portrayed as the upwards striving intellectual who loses out in the game of high politics. It was a period when Brecht's *Galileo* was playing with great success in Milan and the theatre was a subject of intense debate in the intellectual and political ferment leading up to the unrest of 1968. For Fo the most important result was probably his collaboration with a group of left-wing musicians who had become interested in the political potential of popular songs. Their work appealed to him because he was himself 'interested above all in a past attached to the roots of the people… and the concept of 'the new in the traditional'. They put together a show, built round popular and radical songs, to which Fo contributed his theories on the importance of gesture and rhythms in the performance of folksong; it marked an important step in his development.

In 1967 he put on his last production for the bourgeois theatre, *La signora è da buttare* (The Lady is Discardible), in which a circus was made the vehicle for an attack on the United States and capitalist society in general. It again attracted the attention of the authorities. Fo was called to police headquarters in Milan and threatened with arrest for 'offensive lines', not included in the approved version, attacking a head of state – Lyndon Johnson. By now it was becoming 'more and more difficult to act in a theatre where everything down to the subdivision of the seating… mirrored the class divisions. The choice for an intellectual,' Fo concluded, 'was to leave his gilded ghetto and put himself at the disposal of the movement.'

The company with which the Fo's confronted this task was the cooperative Nuova Scena – an attempt to dispense with the traditional roles in a stage company and to make decision-making collective. It was, Fo said in retrospect, a utopian project in which individual talents and capabilities were sacrificed to egalitarian principles. But whatever the internal difficulties there was no doubt as to the success the company enjoyed with a new public which it sought out in the working-class estates, in cooperatives and trade union halls, in factories and workers' clubs. It was a public which knew nothing of the theatre but which found the political attitudes the company presented close to its experience of life. Each performance was followed by a discussion.

Nuova Scena did not last long – it was torn apart by political arguments, by arguments over the relationship of art to society and politics, and by questions of organisation. There were also difficulties with the Communist Party, which often controlled the premises used and whose officials began to react negatively to satirical attacks on their bureaucracy, the inflexibility of the Party line, the intolerance of real discussion. Before the split came, the company had put on a *Grande pantomima con bandiere e pupazzi medi e piccoli* (Grand Pantomime with Flags and Little and Medium Puppets), in which Fo used a huge puppet, drawn from the Sicilian tradition, to represent the state and its continual fight with the 'dragon' of the working class. But the most important production was Fo's one-man show *Mistero Buffo*, which was to become one of his enduring triumphs in Italy and abroad. In it he drew on the counter culture of the Middle Ages, on apocryphal gospel stories, on legend and tales, presenting episodes in which he played all the roles and used a language in part invented, in part archaic, in part drawn from the dialects of Northern Italy. It has been described as 'an imaginary Esperanto of the poor and disinherited'. In performing the scenes of which *Mistero Buffo* is composed – such as the resurrection of Lazarus, the marriage at Cana, Pope Boniface's encounter with Jesus on the Via Dolorosa and others – Fo drew on two main traditions: that of the *giullare*, the travelling comic, singer, mime, who in the Middle Ages was the carrier of a subversive culture; and that of the great clowns of the Commedia dell'Arte with their use of masks, of dialect and of *grammelot*, that extraordinary onomatopoeic rendering of a language – French, say – invented by the fifteenth-century comedians in which there are accurate sounds and intonations but few real words, all adding up (with the aid of highly expressive mime) to intelligible discourse.

When Nuova Scena split in 1970 it came hard on the heels of mounting polemics in the Communist press. Looking back, Franca Rame has admitted that she and Dario Fo were perhaps sectarian and sometimes mistaken but that they had had to break with the Communist cultural organisations if they wished to progress. The result was La Comune, a theatre company with its headquarters in Milan. The Fo's were now politically linked to the new Left, which found the Communist Party too authoritarian, too locked in the mythology of the Resistance, too inflexible and increasingly conservative. In *Morte accidentale di un'anarchico* (Accidental Death of an Anarchist) Fo produced a piece in which his skill at writing farce and his gifts as a clown were put brilliantly at the service of his politics, playing on the tension between the real death of a prisoner and the farcical inventions advanced by the authorities to explain it. It is estimated that in four years the piece was seen by a million people, many of whom took part in fierce debates after the performance. Fo had succeeded in his aim of making of the theatre 'a great machine which makes people laugh at dramatic things… In the laughter there remains a sediment of anger.' So no easy catharsis. There followed a period in which Fo was deeply engaged politically – both through his writings and through his involvement with Franca Rame, who was the main mover of the project – in Red Aid, which collected funds and comforts for Italian political prisoners detained in harsh conditions. His writing dealt with the Palestinian struggle, with Chile, with the methods of the Italian police. In the spring of 1973 Franca Rame was kidnapped from her home in Milan by a Fascist gang, raped and left bleeding in the street. Fo himself later that year was arrested and held in prison in Sardinia for refusing to allow police to be present at rehearsals. Demonstrations and protests ensured his release. Dario Fo had, as his lawyer said, for years no longer been only an actor but a political figure whom the state powers would use any weapon to silence.

His political flair was evident in the farce *Non si paga, non si paga* (Can't Pay? Won't Pay!) dating from 1974, which deals with the question of civil disobedience. Significantly, the main upholder of law and order is a Communist shop steward, who disapproves of his wife's gesture of rebellion against the rising cost of living – a raid on a supermarket. It was a piece tried out on and altered at the suggestion of popular audiences – a practice Fo has often used. It was the same spirit that inspired his *Storia della tigre* (The Tale of a Tiger), an allegorical monologue dating from 1980 – after a trip to China, and based on a Chinese folktale – the moral of which is that, if you have 'tiger' in you, you must never delegate responsibility to others, never expect others to solve your own problems, and above all avoid that unthinking party loyalty which is the enemy of reason and of revolution. In 1981, following on the kidnapping of Aldo Moro came *Clacson, trombette e pernacchi* (Trumpets and Raspberries). In it Fo doubled as Agnelli, the boss of FIAT, and a FIAT shop steward, whose identities become farcically confused. The play mocks the police and their readiness to see terrorists everywhere and the political cynicism which led to Moro's being abandoned to his fate by his fellow-politicians.

It was the last of Fo's major political works to date. Looking for new fields at a time when the great political upsurge has died away and the consumerist state has apparently triumphed, Fo has turned in recent years to a play on Elizabeth and Essex, with a splendid transvestite part for himself which allows him to use the dialect of *Mistero Buffo*, and a Harlequinade – a slight but charming piece that returns to the techniques of the Commedia dell'Arte.

Meanwhile Franca Rame, who has progressively established herself as a political figure and a powerful feminist, has produced a number of one-woman plays, partly in collaboration with her husband – monologues which are a direct political intervention in a society where the role of women is notably restricted by the Church, the state and male traditions. Like all their work the one-woman plays such as *Il risveglio* (Waking Up) or *Una donna sola* (A Woman Alone) depend on the tension between the unbearable nature of the situation in which the female protagonist finds herself and the grotesque behaviour of people around her – in particular the men. It is a theme which is treated with anger and disgust in

Lo stupro (The Rape), tragically in her version of *Medea* and comically in *Coppia aperta* (Open Couple) in which the hypocrisies of 'sexual liberation' are dissected.

Dario Fo and Franca Rame have a world-wide reputation. The Scandinavian countries were among the first to welcome them as performers and to produce their work. The whole of Western Europe has by now acknowledged their importance and virtuosity. Ironically the Berliner Ensemble, the theatre foundèd by Brecht to whom Fo owes so much, found Fo's rock version of *The Beggar's Opera* too difficult to take in spite of Brecht's advice to treat famous authors with disrespect if you have the least consideration for the ideas they express. It had to be staged in Italy. Foreign travel has not been without its problems: attacks on the theatre where they played in Buenos Aires under military rule and a visa to the United States was withheld until 1986.

That Fo's work has not lost its power to upset the authorities was demonstrated in December 1987 when – in a peak-time show on Italian television – he introduced his piece *The First Miracle of the Infant Jesus* with remarks about the Church which drew a protest from the Italian hierarchy. Fo's comment was that they were simply frightened that people might laugh at them. In the same programme, Franca Rame's performance of *The Rape* to a mass audience reopened the political question of who instigated the attack on her in 1973. Shortly afterwards Fo mounted a new production in Milan of *Accidental Death of an Anarchist* in protest at the proposal by the city council to remove the memorial plaque to Pinelli, the anarchist whose death at the hands of the police inspired Fo to write the play. For both Dario Fo and Franca Rame theatre is, by its nature, an intervention.

******

Mistero Buffo is one of Dario Fo's most important and celebrated pieces. Its title, which may be translated as *Comic Mystery*, contains a complex of references. One is to early dramatic representations based on Bible stories or lives of the saints of which the English miracle plays and the

French *Miracles de Notre-Dame* are examples. Another, according to Fo, is to the mysteries celebrated in the Mass. It is difficult to believe that there is not also a reference to Mayakovsky's *Misteriya Buff* – a title usually translated into French as *Mystère Bouffe* – the 'heroic, epic and satiric picture of our era' which Meyerhold staged in October 1918 to celebrate the first anniversary of the October Revolution. It is a mixture of the sacred and the burlesque, which draws on popular traditions and on the medieval mystery plays, finding in the story of the Flood an analogue to the Revolution. On yet another level, *Mistero Buffo* recalls the *opera buffa* – the comic opera – which in 19th century Italy complemented the *opera seria* or *opera lirica*. *Mistero Buffo* bears the marks of the left-wing radicalism of the 1960's, the subversion of accepted wisdom and the challenging of entrenched authorities, which throughout Europe inspired the student movement and was accompanied, particularly in Italy, by large-scale strikes and working-class demonstrations. As first performed in 1969 in a variety of workers' clubs, *Mistero Buffo* was a didactic piece – an illustrated lecture with slides – in which Fo discussed and illustrated the work and function of the medieval *giullare*, a name which is inadequately rendered in English as 'jester' and better rendered (as in this translation) by the French *jongleur* – the strolling performer of the Middle Ages who might be musician, juggler, acrobat, reciter of literary works, or all together.

To Fo the *jongleur* is the embodiment of the disrespect which found expression in the licensed jester in masquerades like the instalment of the Boy Bishops or the Lords of Misrule of Twelfth Night. This irreverence is a common element in medieval art – one has only to think of the explicitly sexual carvings tucked away in certain great cathedrals. It is found in the French *Miracles*, which treated kings, emperors and even the Pope with considerable disrespect. It is reflected, too, in the comic elements of the English mystery plays which have shepherds who are also sheep-stealers and which make comic play with Noah's drunkenness. 'The *jongleur*,' Fo has said in a passage which sums up his own view of the theatre, 'went from place to place, clowning in the square in pieces which were grotesque attacks on the powerful... The *jongleur* was a figure who came from the people, and who from the people drew anger and transmitted it through the medium of the grotesque. For the people the theatre has always been the chief medium of expression, of communication, but also of provocation and agitation through ideas. The theatre is the spoken newspaper of the people in dramatic form.'

The pieces which make up the *Mistero Buffo* are drawn from a variety of sources. They include the works of medieval Italian writers and performers – *The Morality Play of the Blind Man and the Cripple*, for example, or *The Birth of the Villeyn* – anonymous pieces from Italy, Yugoslavia, and elsewhere in Europe, as well as the sacred representations preserved in Czechoslovakia and Poland. All this material has been worked over, adapted and added to by Fo to create a vehicle for his very specific genius as an actor and writer, who in some cases has developed an idea, a hint, in the original, into a dramatic piece – for example, *The Birth of the Jongleur*. There have been criticisms of his use of the material and doubts as to the authenticity of certain texts, but his success in creating a work which has been shaped into performance by an unrivalled mime and actor makes such criticisms irrelevant. When playing them Fo performs alone on a bare stage, a microphone in hand, without make-up, wearing a polo-neck and dark trousers in a performance lasting up to three hours, which provides a true example of what Brecht meant by 'alienation'. It is a method of working which has had an extraordinary resonance wherever he has appeared and attracted huge audiences – but the greatest were those in Italy, such as the estimated 30,000 people who gathered in the open air in Milan in 1974 to see *Mistero Buffo*.

The framework in which the texts are set is less rigidly didactic than it was in the 1969 version. Through it – frequently in interaction with the audience – Fo develops his theories about the role of the *jongleur* and the origins of the synthetic language in which the pieces are written: a construct from the dialects of the Po Valley and archaisms. To the original texts he has added stories drawn from the apocryphal

Gospels in which the figure of Jesus embodies a version of Christianity that reflects the heretical views of certain medieval sects – sects which saw in his teachings a challenge to the rich and the powerful and an attack on the established social order. For Fo the material on which he draws is evidence of the importance of an alternative popular culture which found expresson through the *jongleur*.

Fo's interpretation of history, his views on the sub-culture of the Middle Ages and the role of the *jongleur* in propagating it, together with what is seen as his anti-intellectualism, have not gone unchallenged. But Fo brushes such criticisms aside as modern expressions of a dominant culture. He is above all not interested in academic historical reconstruction. 'When I reproduce the way in which the *jongleur* caused the Bible and the Gospels to be read, I am showing the people today how the people then used to discover in the culture of those times... the fate that awaited them – the way in which it expressed itself through the mouth of the *jongleurs* – and I invite them to reappropriate *their own* culture so as to be able to confront again, today, academic culture based on books.' His political thrust is clear as is the Italian tradition on which he bases himself. It is that of Gramsci, the Italian communist politician and theoretician, who died in Mussolini's prison and from whom Fo quotes in the introduction to the first edition of *Mistero Buffo*: 'To know oneself means to be oneself, means to be one's own master, to find oneself, to step out of chaos, to be an element of order, but of one's own order and one's own discipline in the service of an ideal... If it is true that universal history is a chain of efforts which humanity has made to liberate itself from privileges and from prejudices and from idolatries, one cannot see why the proletariat, which wishes to add another link to that chain, should not know how and by whom it has been preceded and what benefit it can derive from that knowledge.'

STUART HOOD
December 1987

Translator's Note

Fo originally played these pieces in dialect (an aspect of his theatrical enterprise that often goes unnoticed when his works appear in translation). As Stuart Hood shows in the Appendix to this book, the pieces can also be translated in dialect form.

My brief, however, was to produce a translation in standard English, suitable for reading as a playtext, but also suitable for performance. This translation was in fact used by the 1982 Theatre Company in their memorable ensemble performance of *Mistero Buffo* at Riverside Studios in 1983.

In translating the words *giullare* and *villano*, I have used two words introduced into English by the Normans and current in the times of Chaucer: *jongleur* and *villeyn*. I have tended to use 'the people' to render *il popolo* (a term which has a political connotation). I have rendered *Mistero Buffo* as *The Comic Mysteries*.

The text as published in this edition is drawn from the 1977 Bertani version; some of Fo's introductory material about Italian cultural history is not included here.

ED EMERY

MISTERO BUFFO
The Comic Mysteries

ACTOR: The term 'mystery' was already in use by the second and third centuries AD. It means a play, a religious representation, a performance.

We still hear the term used nowadays, during the mass, when the priest says: 'In the first glorious mystery... in the second mystery... etc.' The word 'mystery' means 'a religious performance'; comic mystery, on the other hand, means a grotesque performance.

The comic mysteries were invented by the people.

As far back as the second and third centuries after Christ, people used to entertain themselves (and this was not merely a form of entertainment) by playing, performing dramas in a form which was both grotesque and laden with irony. The reason for this was that, for the people, the theatre, and especially grotesque theatre, has always been a primary means of expression, of communication, and also a vehicle for the development and spreading of ideas. The theatre was the spoken and dramatised newspaper of the people of that time.

The *jongleur* used to turn up in the streets of the town, and reveal to the people their own condition — that of being beaten as well as being taken for a ride. Because the law prescribed beatings as well as hangings. There were plenty of other examples of vicious laws like this. Anyway, the *jongleur* was a figure who, in the Middle Ages, was part of the people. As Muratori[1] says, the *jongleur* was born from the people, and from the people he took their anger in order to be able to give it back to them, mediated via the grotesque, through 'reason', in order that the people should gain greater awareness of their own condition. And it is for this reason that in the Middle

1. Muratori: 18th century Italian scholar.

Ages, *jongleurs* were killed with such abandon; they flayed them alive, they cut out their tongues, not to mention other niceties of the time.

Photo 1: A *Buffonata*.

But now let us return to the 'Comic Mysteries'. Here (photo 1) we have a picture showing a scene of buffoonery, a procession preceding one of the ironic-grotesque performances. We see the people also taking part, dressed up in fancy dress. It is clear that the figures portrayed here are ordinary people, dressed up in *mammuttones*. What does *mammuttones* mean? They were an extremely ancient design of mask, half goat and half devil. In Sardinia today it is still possible to see peasants wearing these extraordinary masks during particular festivals. As you can see from the slide, they are almost all portrayed as devils. Here we have a *jongleur* portraying the Joker, the Fool (a popular allegorical figure), and here we have another Devil... and another...

Here (photo 2), further along, we see devils, witches, and a picturesque passing friar. Another particular that you should note is that everyone has instruments for making noises. The business of making a din, a racket, was an essential part of those festivals. (*He points to one of the figures*) This person is carrying a *ciucciué* – one of the names they give it in Naples. This is a pair of special leather bellows. When you squeeze them, they give out a tremendous farting noise. (*He points to another figure on the slide*) This fellow with his leg half cocked doesn't need a fart-machine. As you can see, he makes his own

Photo 2: A *Buffonata*.

noises... He's a naturalist... So, here you have all these people making a racket. These folk would put on their masks, and gather in the street, whereupon they would set up a kind of make-believe trial of the noblemen, the rich, the powerful, and bosses in general. In other words, merchants, emperors, grasping moneylenders, bankers... all of which anyway amount to more or less the same thing. Bishops and cardinals were also included.

I really can't imagine why, in the Middle Ages, they put bishops and cardinals together with the rich and powerful.... This was a particularly striking element of these performances, but we have not yet tracked down the reasons! Obviously, the bishops and the rich people in question were make-

believes... For some curious reason, real rich people prefer-
red not to come down and join in people's fun on these occa-
sions. The make-believe noblemen were dressed to fit the
part. A kind of trial took place, amid scenes of some violence,
and on the basis of specific charges. 'You did such and such...
You have exploited... You have robbed... You have killed...
etc.' The crowning moment of this performance was a big
bonfire, into which all these rich people and noblemen were
hurled, with imaginary pots of boiling oil poured over them,
and they were subjected to make-believe executions and skin-
ning alive.

Obviously, real rich people used to stay at home on days
like this, because, who knows, they might have been walking
down the street and... gotcha! 'Oh, excuse me, I thought you
were only a make-believe rich person.' So, in order to avoid
being taken for make-believe rich people, they stayed locked
up in their houses. In fact, there is an interesting if slightly mischievous theory of a major French historian, by name of
Bloch,[1] who came from Alsace and who was killed by the
Nazis for being a Communist. Bloch maintained that slatted
shutters for windows were invented precisely in that period, in
order to enable the rich to watch these demonstrations in the
streets of the city without being seen from below.

On the final day of the festival, all these people, the
jongleurs and the buffoons, would process into church. In the
Middle Ages, the church still had its original character as an
ecclesia – in other words, a meeting place. So, the people
entered this meeting place. This would be at the end of eight
to eleven days of buffoonery, which took place in December
and maintained a continuity with the traditions of the Roman
Fescennine[2] festivals, the Roman carnival. So, the people
entered the church, and there, in the transept, stood the
bishop. The bishop would remove all his trappings, and hand
them over to the chief *jongleur*. The chief *jongleur* then went
up into the pulpit, and began to preach, imitating the bishop's

1. M. Bloch: French scholar and authority on Middle Ages.
2. From Fescennia, a town in Etruria, famous in classical times for
scurrilous dialogues in verse (OED).

own style of preaching. He would imitate not only the bishop's mannerisms and his style, but also the content of his sermons. In other words, he stripped bare the whole mystification and hypocrisy; he revealed the operations of power for what they were.

The *jongleurs* were very good at imitating the style of priestly hypocrisy and paternalism. In fact it is said that San Zeno of Verona was so well taken off by one of the *jongleurs*, so well imitated, that for six months afterwards, every time he tried to go up into his pulpit to preach his sermon, he never once succeeded in getting to the end; after the first three or four sentences, he would begin stuttering, and would have to leave. You would have the following scene. He would begin: 'My beloved faithful, I am here, as a humble shepherd...' And everyone would begin sniggering. 'The Sheep...' 'Baaaah!!' The poor devil would find himself covered in confusion and forced to flee the scene.

Now, in the next picture (photo 3) we see two figures. They are two *milites*.[1] This is a picture of a mosaic to be found in a church in Milan. It's a part of the floor mosaic in the church of Sant'Ambrogio, and even I, when I was an architecture student and had to go and work on this mosaic, never noticed this amazing bit. These figures represent two *jongleurs*, two *jongleurs* dressed as *milites*, as you can see from the theatrical nature of their gestures.

The *milites* found themselves in the popular firing line fairly frequently, because they were particularly hated by the people. Basically, the *milites* consisted of those professional agents of law and order whom today we know as the *police*. With a bit of imagination, you can remove their medieval dress and re-dress them in modern clothes, and you will see how well their faces fit the part.

On your left is a building; this building is not part of the theatrical stage portrayed; it is part of another scene. As you can see, this building outside the arch is made up of several storeys; it has four, five, six floors. Now, we have made inquiries and carried out profound historical researches, and

1. *Milites*: Literally 'soldiers'.

we have discovered that in the Middle Ages, police stations were all built on one floor only. This was in order to guard

Photo 3: *Milites*, from a twelfth-century mosaic in the church of Sant'Ambrogio Milan.

against dipsonomy, a disease which has been known to strike, in particular, policemen and officers of the law. It is a curious disease, whereby during interrogation sessions, they sometimes make mistakes in giving directions. Confusion sets in and they begin to mistake their left for their right. They say: 'You're free to go now... There's the door', and they point to the window! This has happened several times... but only in the Middle Ages, of course.[1]

While we're on the subject of making jokes out of things that are extremely serious and dramatic, yesterday I got a letter from a comrade, a lawyer, saying that allusions like this, to certain events that have happened recently in our country,

Photo 4: 'Fourteenth-century travelling players', Cambrai library.

which are presented here in order to make people laugh, had *upset* him. Well, that is precisely what we intended. In other words, we wanted to make people understand that this was the element which both permits and permitted (in the *jongleur* tradition) the popular actor, the folk player, to scratch people's consciousness, to leave them with a taste of something burned and bitter. The reference to pyres is purely by-the-by.

If I limited myself just to acting out oppression, in the tragic mode, employing rhetoric or melancholy or drama, I would

1. This is a reference to the death of the anarchist Pinelli who "fell" from a window while being interrogated by the Milan police – the story that inspired *Accidental Death of an Anarchist*.

only move my audience to indignation. Inevitably, the message would be lost like water off a duck's back.

I wanted to make this point because I often hear people asking why we should 'laugh' at things that are so serious.

This is something which, precisely, the people have taught us. Speaking of the people, we should remember what Mao Tse-tung says about satire. He says that satire is the most powerful weapon that the people have ever had in order to make clear to themselves, within their own culture, all the misdeeds and corruption of their rulers.

Let's proceed with the slides. In this picture (photo 4) you see another religious performance, which this time is both dramatic and grotesque. This is a performance in Flanders,

Photo 5: Comic-grotesque performance in Antwerp city
    square (1465).

around the year 1360 (the date is inscribed on the print). As you can see, here we have a woman with a lamb in her arms. I am pointing this out now because it will become relevant during a piece that follows later, the 'Slaughter of the Innocents'.

Here too (photo 5) we have a fairly important picture. Here we are in Antwerp in 1465, which was the year prior to the Edict of Toledo.

The Edict of Toledo forbade the people to take part in comic mysteries. The picture speaks for itself, in the sense of explaining why this censorship was necessary. If you look, here you see an actor representing Jesus Christ. Here you have two ruffians. Over there, you have a town crier, who would have been one of the actors, and the people, in front of the stage, react and respond to the crier.

What is the crier saying? He is shouting: 'Who do you want to be crucified? Jesus Christ or Barabbas?' And down below, the people reply by shouting: 'Jean Gloughert!' – who was the Mayor of the city. As you can imagine, little ironies like this, expressed so pointedly and directly, were not calculated to please the Mayor and his friends... Obviously, they began to think: 'Wouldn't it be better if we banned these performances?' Here, in the next slide (photo 6), we have another performance, which is perhaps a little more violent.

Here we are in Paris, in the Place du Louvre, around the same period. If you look, you can see Jesus Christ, an actor playing the part of Christ, together with other actors. Here we have Pontius Pilate, with his little bowl all ready so that he can wash his hands, and here we have two bishops. Note that they are two Catholic bishops. Strictly speaking, they should have been dressed at least in Hebrew dress, don't you think? They should really have been dressed completely differently: pudding basin haircuts, curling sidelocks, clothes of another era, which the people would have recognised as such.

Instead, the people went ahead and stuck two bishops there, dressed in the clothes of our very own Catholic bishops! In other words, they were saying: 'Alright, all this happened in Palestine, agreed, and at that period there weren't yet any Christians, and obviously those priests up there would have

Photo 6: A Passion Play. Place du Louvre, Paris (fifteenth century).

been Hebrews, and so they would have been of another religion, another reality! Yes, admitted. But at the same time, they
were still two bishops, those who insisted on Jesus Christ
being sent to the cross. And the fact is that, throughout the
ages, bishops have always taken the rulers' side when it comes
down to it, and end up sending poor sods like us to the cross!'

Naturally, sentiments like these were not pleasing to the
Pope, let alone to the bishops and cardinals. So they decided
to hold a conference in Toledo. They said: 'That's enough! We
can no longer permit a situation where the people use this kind
of theatre – where they start with religion and then turn everything into burlesque and irony.'

And so they banned the representation not only of the Gospels, but also of the Bible as a whole.

Speaking of the ways in which bible stories turned to effect, here (photo 7) we have a picture of a *jongleur*. He is enacting

Photo 7: 'King David's drinking session', from a medieval manuscript.

David's famous drinking session. In the Bible, it relates that David went on a drinking session that lasted for seven days. Remarkable! During this time, he picked on just about everybody in sight. He began by insulting his father, his mother, and the Holy Father, but in particular he picked on his own subjects, in other words, the people. He said, more or less: 'You people, vulgar, wretched, and also a bit stupid, why do you believe all these stories?'

The *jongleur* enacted all this in the grotesque, and shouted to his audience: 'But do you really believe that the Holy Father came down to earth and said: "Right, that'll do with all these arguments about division of wealth and land. I'm going to sort it out, I'll sort everything out. Right, you, you with the beard, come here, I like you. Take this crown: you can be king. You... come here. And your wife? You're nice, you can be queen. Oh, what an ugly face you've got... here, you can be Emperor. What about that fellow over there... He looks pretty crafty... Come on, come on, you can be bishop. As for you, you're going to be a merchant. And you, come on, come on... you see that, all that territory, all that land that stretches to the river over there... that's all yours... I like you... But be sure that you hold on to it! Don't ever let anyone else get their hands on it, and make sure that you work it well. And you too... Here's some land for you... That fellow's a relative of yours, you say...? That's good! That way you can keep everything in the family! Now, let's see... you can have all that bit over by the sea. Fishing rights, on the other hand, go to you... And you, down there, miserable shrivelled wretches that you are, you, and you, and you, and you, and also your wives, you're going to *work* for him... and for him... and for him... and also for him... And if you complain, I shall hurl you into Hell, otherwise my name is not God! And it is, by God!"'

Well, performances like this did not at all please the wealthier elements of the community. So, it was decided, or rather the bishops decided, that any *jongleur* who was found uttering such unpleasantnesses before the people was to be burned alive.

However, there was a famous German *jongleur*, one Hans Holden (photo 8), who was extremely good at playing this piece about David's drinking session. He took the liberty of performing the piece after the Edict had been issued. They burned him at the stake. The poor soul believed that the

Photo 8: 'The arrest of Hans Holden'.

bishops were only joking with their threat: 'You don't really think that they're going to put me on a bonfire, do you?' But he was wrong. Bishops are serious people, and they never joke! As I say, they burned him alive. End of story.

During the Middle Ages, there was also a popular technique for drawing people's attention to these particular plays and their performance. Remnants of it are still found today, in Puglia, during the feast of St Nicholas of Bari, a famous bishop, a saint and a black man, who came from the East. Nowadays this festival has been reduced to a fairly normal procession, of people carrying placards which, in the Middle Ages, would have served to indicate the scenes, the performances that were to be enacted that same evening. Bringing up the rear were the *battuti*, the flagellants, who went through the streets flogging themselves like mad. It wasn't for nothing that this was a religious performance!

In addition, when the procession had finished winding its way through the streets and squares of the city, these flagellants would gather around the stage where the performance was to take place, and would chant, shout, lament and even breathe chorally, together, in order to underline the dramatic and grotesque moments of the performance. My reason for bringing this up is because, in the course of the various pieces that I shall perform, you will hear passages of choral chanting. Their chant was more or less along the following lines:

THE FLAGELLANTS' LAUDE

(*Modelled on examples from Pordenone, Brescia and Mantua*)

Ahiiii. Beat yourselves. Beat yourselves. Ahiiiiah!
  Friends, get in line.
  Beat yourselves hard and with good heart.
  Complain not of the pain. Beat yourselves.
  Fear not that you are naked,
  Fear not the whip's lash and the scars it makes,
  The torn and broken flesh.

Ahiiii. Beat yourselves. Beat yourselves. Ahiiiiah!
  If you hope for salvation,
  Beat yourselves with the lash,

With the lash, hear it crack.
Do not flinch. Beat yourselves!
For the Lord Almighty was beaten, in truth!

Ahiiii. Beat yourselves. Beat yourselves. Ahiiiah!
  If you seek to do penance
  And reduce the dread sentence
  That is shortly to come,
  And which nobody can escape – Beat yourselves!
  This sentence hangs over us all,
  So let us beat ourselves. Feel the pain.

Ahiiii. Beat yourselves. Beat yourselves. Ahiiiiah!
  In order to save us from sin
  Jesus Christ was beaten.
  On the cross he was nailed
  And in his face they spat. Beat yourselves!
  And gall was given him to drink!
  And St Peter was not there.

Ahiiii. Beat yourselves. Beat yourselves. Ahiiiiah!
  And you rulers, you usurers,
  You will suffer misfortune,
  For you have spat in the face of Christ,
  Enriching yourselves with ill-gotten gains. Beat yourselves!
  You who have squeezed, as a person would crush grapes,
  The money out of those who sweat and toil.

Ahiiii. Beat yourselves. Beat yourselves! Ahiiiiah!

THE SLAUGHTER OF THE INNOCENTS

Introduction

A few years ago, an extraordinary exhibition was held in the Abbey of Chiaravalle in Milan. It was an exhibition of theatrical machines. These were magnificent statues, whose limbs were articulated so that they moved just like puppets or dolls. The movement was controlled by a series of levers and hooks which were operated by a puppeteer concealed in the rear of the statue (only the front of the statue was figuratively portrayed). One of the exhibits was a magnificent Madonna and Child, dating from the twelfth century, where both the figures were mobile. Their arms, torso, elbow joints and even their eyes moved, by a mechanism which functioned on the *déséquilibre* principle invented by Flemish puppeteers. For example, there was a balance mechanism in the forearm, whereby the hand was articulated, and any movement, however slight, would cause the hand to rotate at the wrist, before then coming to a stop. The slightest impulse would make the hands, or some other part of the body, move with an extraordinary grace. And this really did give the impression of an object come to life.

The same principle underlies the construction of another famous statue, the Christ of Aquileia. The mechanism cannot be seen, because clothing covers the statue's whole body; but when the garment is removed, you can see that the whole body is articulated, from the head on downwards.

Now, why was it that the people, when they put their plays on, decided to use these machines in order to represent the godhead. Were they perhaps worried about being blasphemous, scared of encroaching on the sacredness of the divine person? No! Not at all. It was done because the actor, the player, wanted his audience to focus their attention not on the divine presence, but on the man. If an actor had been seen to come on stage wearing a costume depicting Jesus Christ, he would have drawn everyone's attention to himself. On the other hand, the statue could be present as something purely indicative and symbolic, and the player had space to develop and emphasise the dramatic content of the *human* condition: desperation, hunger and pain.

I have gone into the question of theatrical machines because the piece which I am now going to perform does in fact require the use of a machine portraying the Madonna with the Child in her arms. In this piece another woman also figures, a crazy woman, who holds a lamb in her arms – and this is why I mentioned previously that Flemish picture, in which you see a woman with a lamb in her arms. This woman's baby had been killed during the Slaughter of the Innocents, and she found a lamb in a sheep-pen; she took it in her arms and went around telling everybody that this was her own baby. The allegory behind this is clear: the lamb is the *agnus dei*, the Lamb of God, the Son of God, and so this woman is also the Madonna.

This double-play of the Woman/Madonna figure is extremely ancient. In fact, it comes from the Greeks. The Woman is in a position to say things which a real Madonna, an actress playing the Madonna (or rather, an actor, as was the custom in those days) would never have been able to say. This woman goes so far as to curse God, with an incredible violence. With her lamb in her arms, she begins to shout: '...Why didn't you keep your son with you, if you knew that he was going to cause us so much suffering, so much pain! Your turn will come, to understand the suffering of mankind, you who tried to enact this exchange to your advantage... For one little cup of blood you have caused a river of blood to flow... A thousand babies killed for your one single child. Why didn't you keep your child with you, if you knew he was going to cost us so much suffering, so much pain! You will come to see pain too, the pain, the desperation of mankind, on the day when you too will see your son die – on the Cross. On that day, you will understand the tremendous suffering you have imposed on mankind, for a sin and by an error! No father on earth, however ill-meaning, would ever have thought to impose this on his own son. No matter how evil that father was!'

This is certainly an outrageous blasphemy! It is like saying: 'Eternal father, you are the scum of all scum! No father on earth could ever be as evil as you.' And why should the people feel such a deep-seated hatred towards the Eternal Father? We have already seen why. Because the Eternal Father represents the impositions which rulers have forced upon the people; it is he who introduced divisions among the people, who gave land, power and privilege to certain groups of people, and handed out suffering, desperation, subjection, humiliation and mortification to the rest. This is why God is hated, because he represents the rulers; it is he who hands out thrones and privileges. On the other hand, Jesus Christ is loved, because it is he who came to earth seeking to give people back their Spring. Above all else he represents dignity, and in these folk traditions the question of dignity is raised over and over again, with an incredible persistence. Dignity…

Now let us move on to the piece representing the *Slaughter of the Innocents*.

Before I start, I would like to draw your attention to one thing, the dialect (or rather the language) of the piece. It is a 13/15th century Lombard dialect, but reworked by an actor who, in the course of a week, might find himself moving from one village to another, from one town to the next. One day he might be in Brescia, the next in Verona, and then in Bergamo, etc etc. So, he would find himself having to play the piece in dialects that were quite different from each other. There were hundreds of dialects in those days, with considerable differences between them, even between neighbouring cities. Thus, the *jongleur* would need to know hundreds of dialects. So what did he do? He invented one of his own, a language formed from many dialects, and containing the possibility of substituting key words. Should he find himself in a moment of difficulty, not knowing which precise word to choose in order to convey his meaning, you would find him giving three, maybe four, even five synonyms.

There is a striking example of this: a *jongleur* from Bologna tells the tale of a girl who came to kiss a man whom she loved. But suddenly she was afraid. She wanted to make love with him, but when it came to the delicate moment, she suddenly pushed him away, and said: *Non me toccar a mi, che mi a son zovina, son fiola, tosa son e garsonetta*. In other words, she said: 'I am a girl, I am a girl, I am a girl, I am a girl.' All the words he used mean simply 'girl'. And his audience could simply pick out the word that they understood best.

In the piece that follows, in the original text, you will find many of these reiterations. But they are also used with another purpose in mind: in order to increase the poetic content of the moment, and, particularly, to expand its dramatic content. This is something quite unique to the art of the *jongleur*, to the theatre of the people – the ability to choose and select words and sounds that are best fitted to the moment. This is why you hear, for example, *croz*, *cros*, *crosge*, etc, all of which mean *croce* or 'cross', and each of which is taken from different dialects in order to give the best feeling to what is being enacted on the stage. The piece is performed by only one player, and afterwards I shall explain why. This is not to do with exhibitionism; it has an important underlying rationale. There will also be a moving statue onstage, as I explained, as well as the chorus of flagellants which opens the piece. At a certain point, as you will see, a soldier is killed on stage, and the flagellants' chorus sings a funeral dirge.

THE SLAUGHTER OF THE INNOCENTS

CHORUS OF FLAGELLANTS:
Ahiii! Beat yourselves. Beat yourselves! Ahiiiiah!
With pain and lamentation
For the slaughter of the innocents,
A thousand innocent children.
They killed them like lambs.
From their fear-stricken mothers
King Herod plucked them.
Ahiiii! Beat yourselves. Beat yourselves! Ahiiiiah!

WOMAN: Pig, murderer, don't touch my baby.

SOLDIER: Let it go, let go of that baby, or I'll cut your hands off... I'll kick you in the belly... Let go...

WOMAN: Nooo! Kill me instead... (*The* SOLDIER *snatches her baby and kills it*) Ahiiii, ahiiii, you've killed him! Dead!

SOLDIER: Hey, here comes another one. Stop where you are, Woman, or I shall run both of you through, you and your baby!

WOMAN: Run us both through, I would rather you did...

SOLDIER: Don't be crazy... You're still young, you have time enough to have a dozen more children... Give me that one... Don't make a fuss!

WOMAN: No! Get your dirty hands off him.

SOLDIER: Ouch! Bite me, would you? So, take that! And drop that bundle.

WOMAN: Have pity, I pray you... Don't kill him. I'll give you all that I have.

The SOLDIER *seizes her bundle and finds that it's a lamb.*

SOLDIER: What's this, eh? An animal, a lamb?

WOMAN: Oh yes! It's not a baby... It's a lamb... I don't have any children... I can't have children... Oh, Soldier, I pray you, don't kill my lamb... Because it's not yet Easter, and you would commit a great sin if you kill him!

SOLDIER: Look, woman, are you trying to play a joke on me... Or are you crazy, perhaps?

WOMAN: Me, crazy? No, I am not crazy!

Another SOLDIER *joins in.*

SOLDIER II: Come on, leave her lamb alone... The poor woman is out of her mind with grief because we've killed her son. What's the matter with you? Come on, there's still a lot more to be killed.

SOLDIER I: Wait, I think I'm going to be sick...

SOLDIER II: What do you expect! You eat like a pig –

onions, salted mutton, stuff like that, and afterwards… Come over here, there's a tavern on the corner. I'll buy you a nice stiff drink.

SOLDIER I: No. It's not because of what I've eaten… It's because of this butchery, this slaughter of the children that we've been doing. That's what's turned my stomach.

SOLDIER II: If you knew you were such a delicate soul, you shouldn't have joined up as a soldier in the first place.

SOLDIER I: I joined up in order to kill enemies, to kill men…

SOLDIER II: And presumably to send a few women tumbling in the hay as well, eh?

SOLDIER I: Yes, maybe… But only if they were enemy women!

SOLDIER II: And butcher their cattle…

SOLDIER I: Only enemy cattle.

SOLDIER II: And burn their houses… And kill their old people, their chickens, their children … Enemy children, of course!

SOLDIER I: Yes, babies too. But only in war! There is no shame and dishonour in war; the trumpets sound, the drums roll, and there are hymns of war, *and* the captains' fine speeches at the end!

SOLDIER II: Oh, you'll get captains' fine speeches at the end of this slaughter too…

SOLDIER I: But here we're killing innocents.

SOLDIER II: What do you mean! Aren't people innocent in wars too? What have those people ever done to you? Have they ever done anything to you, those poor souls whom you kill and maim, to the sound of your trumpets?

A machine representing the MADONNA AND CHILD *passes across the back of the stage.*

SOLDIER II: Well, blind my eyes if that's not the Virgin Mary with her Child, the one we're looking for. Let's grab her before she can get away… Get a move on… This time we'll get that big reward that's been posted.

SOLDIER I: I don't want the dirty, stinking reward.

SOLDIER II: Alright, then, I'll have it all for myself.

SOLDIER I: No, you're not taking it either!

He bars his way.

SOLDIER II: But have you gone mad? Let me pass. We've got orders to kill the Virgin's child!

SOLDIER I: I shit on those orders. Don't move from there, or I'll cut you down!

SOLDIER II: Wretch, don't you understand that if this child lives, he will become King of Galilee in place of Herod? That was what the prophecy said!

SOLDIER I: I shit on Herod and on the prophecy!

SOLDIER II: Alright, so you need to take a shit… Go and do it in a field somewhere, since you've got no stomach for this. Let me pass, because I don't want to lose that reward!

SOLDIER I: No! I've had enough of seeing babies killed!

SOLDIER II: Alright then, so much the worse for you!

He runs him through with his sword.

SOLDIER I: Ahiiii… You've killed me… Wretch… You've run me through!

SOLDIER II: I'm sorry… You were being really stupid… I didn't want to…

SOLDIER I: My blood's pissing out all over… Oh mamma, mamma… Where are you, mother…? It's getting dark… I'm cold, mother… Mamma.

He dies.

SOLDIER II: I never killed him. That one was a corpse from the moment that he began to have pity. As the proverb says: 'A soldier who feels pity is already as good as dead.' And now he's made me lose my chance of capturing the Virgin and her Child.

The FLAGELLANTS *sing a funeral dirge. Exit the*
SOLDIER, *dragging away his companion's body. Enter the*
MADONNA, *or rather the model of the Madonna. Behind
her, enter the* MAD WOMAN.

WOMAN: Don't run away, Madonna… Don't be scared, I'm
not a soldier… I'm a woman… a mother, too, I've got a
baby too. Hide yourself here and rest, because the soldiers
have gone away… Sit down, you poor woman… You look
as if you've been running… Let's see your baby. Oh how
pretty he is. What a bonny colour! How old is he? Pretty,
pretty… Look how happy he is, he's smiling… Pretty,
pretty… He must be just the same age as mine…

What's his name? Jesus? Oh, that's a lovely name:
Jesus… Pretty, pretty… little Jesus. Oh, and he's got two
little teeth… Oh, how lovely. Mine hasn't yet got all his
teeth… He's been a little poorly, over the last month, but
he's better now… Here he is, look, sleeping like a little
angel… (*She calls him by name*) Mark! He's called Mark,
you know. Look how he's sleeping. Oh, my pretty little
one! You're pretty too, my little Mark… You know, it's
true what they say – we mothers always think that our own
babies are the prettiest of all… They might have some little
defect, but we never see it.

You know, I love this little creature so much that if they
were to take him away from me, I would go crazy! When I
think of the terrible fright I had this morning, when I went
to the cradle and found it empty, full of blood, and my baby
nowhere in sight… Luckily, though, it wasn't true…
It was only a dream. I knew it was a dream, because a little
later I woke up, and I was still under the influence of the
dream, and I was so desperate that I almost went out of my
mind! I went out into the courtyard, and I began to curse
God: 'God, awesome in your heartlessness,' I shouted,
'You ordered this slaughter… you wanted this sacrifice in
exchange for sending down your Son: a thousand babies
killed for the sake of one of yours: a river of blood for a
cup! You should have kept him with you, this Son of yours,
if he was going to cost us poor souls such a mighty sacrifice.

Ah, but in the end you too will see what it means to die of heartbreak, the day when your own son dies! In the end, you too will understand what a mighty and awesome affliction you have visited on mankind for all eternity. No father on earth, no matter how wicked, would ever have had the heartlessness to impose such a thing on his own son.'

There I was in the yard, shouting these curses, as I say, when suddenly I looked round, and there, in the sheep pen, in among all the sheep, I discovered my baby, crying... I recognised him instantly, and took him in my arms, and began to cry, along with him. 'I ask your pardon, merciful Lord, for those bad words I shouted... I didn't mean them... It was the Devil, yes, it was the Devil who put them into my mouth! You, Lord, who are so good, you saved my son...! And you have made it so that everyone takes him for a little lamb; and even the soldiers don't realise it, and they let me go. I shall have to be careful when Easter comes, though, because then everybody starts killing lambs the way they've been killing babies today. The butchers will come to me looking for him, but I shall put a bonnet on his head, with all ribbons in it, and everyone will think that he is a baby. But right now I must make sure that nobody recognises him as a baby... In fact I shall take him out to pasture, and I shall make him eat grass, so that everyone thinks that he really is a sheep... And anyway, it will be easier for my son to get by as a sheep than as a man in this wretched world!'

Oh, he's woken up. Look, Madonna, my little Mark... Isn't he pretty... The little flower! (*The* WOMAN *draws her shawl aside and shows the* MADONNA *the lamb. The* MADONNA *shudders*) Oh, Madonna, do you feel ill? Cheer up, don't cry, because the worst is over, and everything will turn out alright, you'll see... Just have faith in Providence, which helps us all!

CHORUS: Lord, who art so full of pity that you make crazy those who are not capable of escaping from their grief...

WOMAN: (*Cradling the lamb and singing*)
    Hushabye, lullaby,
    Mummy's pretty baby.
    The Madonna cradled
    While the angels sang,
    Saint Joseph slept standing,
    And Baby Jesus laughed,
    And Herod cursed,
    A thousand babies flew to heaven.
      Hushabye, lullaby.

THE MORALITY PLAY
OF THE BLIND MAN AND THE CRIPPLE

Introduction

Another piece which relates to the theme of dignity is the
Morality Play of the Blind Man and the Cripple. This piece is

Photo 9: 'Moralité de l'aveugle et du boiteux'. Frontispiece of a
seventeenth-century French broadsheet.

well-known throughout the European medieval theatrical tradition. Versions of it are found in many countries – one in Hainault in Belgium; more than one in France (photo 9); and a well-known version by Andrea della Vigna, in Italy at the end of the fifteenth century.

Anyway, at a certain moment, the blind man says: 'Dignity does not lie in straight legs, or eyes that see; dignity is not having an employer to subject you.' True freedom is the freedom of not having bosses – not only that I should be free, but that I should live in a world that is also free – where others do not have bosses either. Just imagine it – all this in around 1200-1300!

Naturally, we're not taught this kind of thing in school, because it is extremely dangerous to let children know that away back in the Middle Ages poor people had realised a few things… knew that they were being exploited…!

THE MORALITY PLAY
OF THE BLIND MAN AND THE CRIPPLE

THE BLIND MAN: Help me, kind people… Give me alms, because I am a poor unfortunate. I am blind in both eyes, which is perhaps a lesser evil, because if I were able to see myself, I would be overcome with pity for myself, and would go mad with despair.

THE CRIPPLE: Oh, kind-hearted people, take pity on me. I am reduced to such a state. Just the sight of my own body scares me to such an extent that I would run away at top speed, were it not that I, poor cripple, am only able to move in this trolley.

THE BLIND MAN: Just think – I can't move around without forever banging my head on every pillar and post… won't somebody help me?

THE CRIPPLE: Just think – I can't get out of this hole, because the wheels of my little trolley are broken, and I shall end up dying of hunger here if someone doesn't come and help me.

THE BLIND MAN: Once I had a good dog as a companion… but he ran off after a bitch in heat… At least I think it was a bitch, but I can't be sure, because I can't see a thing, me,… maybe it was some lousy rat of a dog or maybe a scabby cat that caused my dog to fall in love.

THE CRIPPLE: Somebody help me… somebody help me… Doesn't someone have four new wheels to lend me for my little trolley? Lord God, I pray you, help to find me four new wheels!

THE BLIND MAN: Whose is that voice, pleading with God because he needs new wheels?

THE CRIPPLE: It is I, the cripple, whose wheels are broken.

THE BLIND MAN: Come over to me, on this side of the street, so that I can see if I can help you… Or rather, no, I can't see… not without a miracle… But anyway, let's see!

THE CRIPPLE: I can't come over to you… May God damn all wheels in the world and turn them square, so that they can no longer go rolling around.

THE BLIND MAN: Ah, if only I could find a way to get over to you… Then you can be sure that I'd happily take you up on my shoulders, all of you, apart from your wheels and your little trolley of course! We two could then become one… which would make us both happy. I would be able to get around with the assistance of your eyes, and you could get around with the aid of my legs.

THE CRIPPLE: Oh, that's an idea! You must have a mighty brain, you! Full of wheels and cogs. I thank the Lord God who has been so gracious as to lend me the wheels of your brain to enable me to get around again and ask for charity!

THE BLIND MAN: Carry on talking, so that I can get my bearings… Is this the right direction?

THE CRIPPLE: Yes. Keep going as you are. You're doing well.

THE BLIND MAN: If I don't want to stumble, it would be better if I came on all fours… There, am I still in the right direction?

THE CRIPPLE: Move over to port a bit... No, not too much! You're moving off-beam. There... drop anchor and back up a bit... Good... Get out the oars, hoist the sail... line her up... Good. Now, full ahead.

THE BLIND MAN: What do you take me for – a galleon? When I get near you, give me your hand.

THE CRIPPLE: Right, I'm holding out both hands! Come on, come on, baby, come to mother... There you are... No...! Don't move to the lee... steer to starboard... Oh my fine lifeboat...

THE BLIND MAN: Do I have you...? Is that really you?

THE CRIPPLE: Yes, it's me, my cock-eyed beauty... Let me hug you!

THE BLIND MAN: I'm dancing with joy, my dear cripple! Come on, I'll take you on board... Get up on my shoulders.

THE CRIPPLE: To be sure, I will... Turn around... Bend down... Now, lift! There we are.

THE BLIND MAN: Ouch, don't dig your knees into my ribs... You're hurting me...

THE CRIPPLE: I'm sorry... It's the first time I've ridden a horse, and I'm not used to it. Now look, you take care that you don't send me tumbling!

THE BLIND MAN: Don't worry, my friend, I've got you as firmly as if you were a sack of turnips. But you, make sure that you do your guide's work properly... Don't send me walking into cow-shit.

THE CRIPPLE: Don't worry, I'll look out. You wouldn't happen to have a piece of iron to put into your mouth, like a bridle, and a pair of reins that I could put around your neck, would you? That way it would be easier for me to guide you around.

THE BLIND MAN: What do you take me for – an ass?! Oh, what a weight you are! Why are you so heavy?

THE CRIPPLE: Lead on...! Save your breath... Giddy-up! Gee up! Trot, my cock-eyed beauty. And pay attention.

When I pull your left ear, you turn to the left… and when I pull…

THE BLIND MAN: Alright, alright, I understand… I'm not an ass. Oh, by God, you're a heavy animal!

THE CRIPPLE: Me, heavy? I'm like a feather… A butterfly.

THE BLIND MAN: A lead butterfly! If I were to drop you, you'd make such a hole in the ground that, God's blood, water would run forth! Did you eat an anvil for your breakfast?

THE CRIPPLE: You must be crazy! It's two days since I last ate.

THE BLIND MAN: Yes, but I'll warrant it's at least two months since you last did a shit.

THE CRIPPLE: Don't talk nonsense. I take God as my witness… It's barely six days since I last performed my needs.

THE BLIND MAN: Six days?! At two meals a day, that makes twelve courses. By Saint Jerome, patron of all porters, I've taken on board a load of provisions sufficient for a year of famine. I'm sorry, but I'm going to have to off-load you here and now, and you will do me the honour of going and emptying your illegal load!

THE CRIPPLE: Stop. Do you hear that noise?

THE BLIND MAN: Yes, it's people shouting and blaspheming! What's making them shout like that?

THE CRIPPLE: Move back a bit, I'll try and see… Back up over there. Good. Now I can see him… They're taking it out on him… Poor creature… Poor Christ…

THE BLIND MAN: What poor Christ?

THE CRIPPLE: Him, Jesus Christ in person… the Son of God.

THE BLIND MAN: The Son of God? Which son?

THE CRIPPLE: What do you mean, which son?! The *only* son, ignoramus! A very holy son… And they say that he has done some amazing, miraculous things; he has cured the worst diseases, the most terrible illnesses known in the world. If you ask me, we'd best get out of these parts as fast as we can!

THE BLIND MAN: Get out? Why?

TIIE CRIPPLE: Because that thought doesn't fill me with joy. They say that if this Son of God even so much as passed by here, I would immediately be miracled. You too...! Just think, if both of us had the misfortune to be relieved of our infirmities! All of a sudden, we would be forced to go out and look for work so as to be able to survive.

THE BLIND MAN: Well, I think that we should go and see this saint, so that he can lift us out of our wretched condition.

THE CRIPPLE: Are you serious? You'll end up getting miracled, and then you'll die of hunger, because everybody will tell you: 'Go to work... '

THE BLIND MAN: Oh, it puts me into a cold sweat just to think of it...

THE CRIPPLE: 'Go to work, vagabond,' they will say. 'People who don't work should go to prison...' And that way you will lose that great privilege which we share with the lords and the masters, of collecting tithes. They use the tricks of the law, and we make use of pity. But both of us take our tolls from fools.

THE BLIND MAN: Let's go. We must avoid meeting this saint... I'd rather die. Oh mother! Let's go... Let's go at the gallop. Grab hold of my ears and lead me as far away as you can from this city! We'll even leave Lombardy... We'll even go to France, or to some other place this Jesus, Son of God, will never get to... I know, we'll go to Rome!

THE CRIPPLE: Calm down... Both of us will be safe and sound... There's no danger yet, because the procession accompanying the saint hasn't moved off yet.

THE BLIND MAN: What are they doing?

THE CRIPPLE: They have tied him to a column… And they're beating him… Oh, how they are beating, they're so worked up.

THE BLIND MAN: Oh, poor boy… Why are they beating him? What has he done to them, for them to get so worked up?

THE CRIPPLE: He has come to tell them about loving each other, about being equal, like so many brothers. But make sure that you don't get taken with compassion for him, because you'll run a great danger of getting miracled.

THE BLIND MAN: No, no, I'm not feeling compassion… That Christ doesn't mean anything to me… I don't know the man. But tell me, what are they doing now…?

THE CRIPPLE: They're spitting on him… Dirty pigs, they're spitting in his face.

THE BLIND MAN: And what's he doing… ? What is he saying, this poor holy son of God?

THE CRIPPLE: He's not saying anything, he's not speaking, he's not fighting back, and he doesn't even look angry with those wicked people…

THE BLIND MAN: And how's he looking at them?

THE CRIPPLE: He's looking at them with looks of pity.

THE BLIND MAN: Oh, dear boy… Don't say another word, because I feel my stomach turning, and a chill on my heart… I fear that it might be something related to compassion.

THE CRIPPLE: I too feel my breath catching in my throat, and my arms shaking… Let's go, let's get away from here.

THE BLIND MAN: Yes, let's go and shut ourselves in some place where you don't have to see unhappy things like this. I know… a tavern… !

THE CRIPPLE: Listen…

THE BLIND MAN: What?

THE CRIPPLE: That noise… It's getting nearer…

THE BLIND MAN: Do you suppose it's the holy Son arriving?

THE CRIPPLE: Oh, dear God! Don't scare me... We would be lost... There's nobody down by that column any more...

THE BLIND MAN: Not even Jesus the Son of God? Where have they all gone?

THE CRIPPLE: Here they are... Look at them all arriving in procession... We're ruined!

THE BLIND MAN: Is the holy man there too?

THE CRIPPLE: Yes, he's in the middle, and they've made him carry a heavy cross, the poor devil!

THE BLIND MAN: Don't wait around here getting all sorry for him... Hurry up instead and get me to some place where we can hide from his eyes.

THE CRIPPLE: Yes, let's go... Go to the right there... Run, run, before he can set eyes on us, this miraculous saint...

THE BLIND MAN: Ouch, I've twisted my ankle... And I can't move any more.

THE CRIPPLE: The devil take you! You have to choose this moment! Couldn't you look where you were putting your feet!

THE BLIND MAN: No, of course I couldn't look, because I'm blind and I can't see my feet! What am I saying, 'I can't see them'? Yes, I *can* see them... I see them! I see my feet... my two lovely feet! By the saints, with all their toes... How many toes? Five per foot... With toenails, big ones and small ones next to each other... Oh, I want to kiss you all, one by one.

THE CRIPPLE: You're mad... Behave yourself, or you'll tip me off... Oh, you've thrown me... Wretch! If I could only give you a good kicking... (*He gives him a kick*) Take that!

THE BLIND MAN: Oh, what a miracle... I can even see the sky... And the trees... And the women (*As if he can see women passing*) How beautiful the women are! ...Well, at least, some of them!

THE CRIPPLE: Hey, was that really me that gave you a kick? Let me try it again: Yes… Yes… Damn this day! I'm ruined!

THE BLIND MAN: Blessed be the holy son that has cured me! I see things that I have never seen in my life… I was a wretched animal to try and run away from him, because there is nothing in the world so sweet and joyful as he.

THE CRIPPLE: The devil take you, and him with you. I must have been really damned unfortunate to get looked at by that man full of love! I'm in despair! I'm going to end up dying with an empty belly… I'm going to end up eating these cured legs of mine, out of sheer anger!

THE BLIND MAN: Now I see it well – I was mad to have wandered off the straight and narrow path to take this dark road… I did not realise what a great prize it was to be able to see! Oh how beautiful the colours are! The eyes of the women, the lips… and the rest… How pretty the ants and flies are… and the sun… I can't wait for the night to come so that I can see the stars and go to the tavern to discover the colour of wine… Thanks be to God, son of God.

THE CRIPPLE: Oh poor me… Now I'll have to go and work for an employer, sweating blood in order to eat… Oh most wretched of wretches! I'm going to have to go and find me another saint who'll do me the favour of making me a cripple once again…

THE BLIND MAN: Miraculous son of God, there are no words either in Latin or in the common tongue which can describe your holiness. Like a river in full flow! Even under the weight of a cross, you still have such an excess of love as to give thought to the misfortunes of poor wretches like us… !

THE MARRIAGE AT CANA

Introduction

In the nineteenth century an Englishman by name of Smith published a book containing illustrations of a number of Italian religious festivals. This, for example, (photo 10) is a picture of a rite which is still performed in Sicily to this day — in Piana dei Greci, to be precise. Here we see Christ's entry into

Photo 10: 'Palm Sunday'. Popular print (nineteenth century).

Jerusalem — you can see him here under the palm branches, surrounded by revellers. The scene reminds one of Bacchus — Dionysus's descent into hell. Dionysus was a Greek god of Thessalo-Minoan origin, dating from some fifteen centuries before Christ. It is said that he so loved mankind that when a demon came to earth and stole the springtime (in order to carry it off to hell and enjoy it all for himself), Dionysus decided to sacrifice himself on mankind's behalf: he mounted a mule, went down to hell, and paid with his own life in order that humanity might have their spring back.

Anyway, fifteen centuries later we find Jesus Christ, coming to earth as a god and seeking to give mankind back their spring. That springtime was, as I have said, man's dignity — a theme that we shall return to later, in another of the pieces I shall perform. And at the heart of the Jesus story we find traces of Bacchus, the god of happiness — of drunkenness even — a jolly, boisterous kind of god.

There is, by the way, nothing unusual about this grafting of one god onto another; it is a familiar characteristic of popular religions.

So, the key character in this jongleur piece is a drunkard. He tells how he went to a wedding feast, and got drunk on wine that had been made by, actually created by, Jesus Christ. Jesus Christ becomes Bacchus; at a certain point he is even shown standing on a table and addressing the wedding guests: "Enjoy yourselves, people; get drunk; have a good time." The important thing is to be happy. Don't wait for heaven after you die, because heaven can be here on earth too. Exactly the opposite of what they ram down your throats when you're kids... that you have to suffer on earth... that it's a vale of tears... that not everybody can be rich, because some people are destined to be poor, and anyway your reward will come in heaven... so relax, and behave yourselves, and don't kick up a fuss... That's more or less the line of argument.

The philosophy that Jesus puts forward in this jongleur piece is quite the opposite. He says: "Get drunk, people... Go ahead, let yourselves go!"

This piece actually involves two characters: the drunkard and an angel. While the angel — or rather the archangel — tries to present the prologue of a religious performance piece, within the traditional style of the genre, the drunkard is bent on mischief. He wants to interrupt the show and tell of how he got magnificently drunk at the Marriage at Cana. The angel speaks in an aristocratic, elegant, polished Venetian dialect;

the drunkard on the other hand speaks in a strong rustic dialect that is crude and highly coloured. I perform this as a solo piece, but not because I'm an exhibitionist: we tried performing it with two actors, but we found it didn't work. You see, almost all these texts were written to be performed by one person. The jongleurs almost always worked on their own; we can see this from the fact that, in the text, things that happen tend to be indicated by the actor splitting himself between two parts, and by allusion, so that the full comic and poetic weight of the piece is heightened by the free play of imagination.

In this piece, you have to use your imagination. Not like when you're watching TV: in order to save you straining your brain, they feed you all the details, all the particulars, and you just sit there, mind half asleep... maybe have a little nap, maybe fart a bit... and the next day you're all fresh and ready for work, all ready to be exploited again.

So: when I'm on this side of the stage (*He points to stage-left*) I shall be the angel, with his fine, aristocratic gestures; when I am over there (*He points to stage-right*) I shall be the drunkard.

For as long as the angel is on stage, the image in photo 11 is projected onto the backdrop.

THE MARRIAGE AT CANA

ANGEL: (*To the audience*) Pay attention, kind people, and I shall tell you of a true story, a story which began...

DRUNKARD: I would like to tell you a story too, about a drinking session, a glorious binge...

ANGEL: Drunkard!

DRUNKARD: I want to tell you...

ANGEL: Silence... Not a word!

DRUNKARD: ...But I...

ANGEL: Silence... I am the one who's supposed to give the prologue! (*To the audience*) Kind people, everything that we are going to tell you will be true, utterly true, and is all taken from books and from the Gospels. Nothing presented here is created from imagination…

Photo 11: A Cimabue angel from Assissi (late fourteenth century).

DRUNKARD: I want to tell a story too, and mine is not imaginary either. I have just been on such a magnificent bender, such a binge, that never again do I ever want to get drunk again, lest I forget how magnificent it was. It was a bender like you've…

ANGEL: Drunkard!

DRUNKARD: I would like to tell…

ANGEL: No… You're not telling anything… Alright?!

DRUNKARD: Ah, but… I…

ANGEL: Ssssh… !

DRUNKARD: But I… No?

ANGEL: Kind people, everything that we are going to tell you is wholly true. Everything comes from books, and from the Gospels. The little imaginary material that we have added…

DRUNKARD: (*Very quietly*) I'll tell you about my wonderful binge afterwards…

ANGEL: Hey! Drunkard!

DRUNKARD: I wasn't doing anything… I only moved my finger.

ANGEL: Well *don't* move your finger!

DRUNKARD: But I don't make any noise with my finger!

ANGEL: You're making a noise… Brrrr!

DRUNKARD: How can I make a noise with my finger?! Alright! I'll do it with my brain… I shall think and think and think, and with my eyes… And they will understand…

ANGEL: No.

DRUNKARD: But I don't make any noise with my brain…

ANGEL: You do make a noise!

DRUNKARD: I make a noise with my brain? Heavens above! I must really be drunk! Holy Mary!

ANGEL: Don't breathe!

DRUNKARD: What, aren't I allowed to breathe? Not even through my nose? I shall burst!

ANGEL: Burst, then!

DRUNKARD: Ah, but if I burst, then I'll make a noise, eh?

ANGEL: Ssssh… !

DRUNKARD: But I…

ANGEL: Everything of what we are about to tell you is true, everything has come from books and from the Gospels. The little imaginary material that we have added…

The DRUNKARD *creeps up on the* ANGEL *and pulls out one of his feathers.*

DRUNKARD: (*Very quietly, miming making the feather fly*) Oh, what a pretty coloured feather!

ANGEL: Drunkard!

DRUNKARD: (*He starts, and mimes swallowing the feather. He coughs*) Eh… But…

ANGEL: Ssssh… !

DRUNKARD: Eh… But I… no…

ANGEL: Everything that we are going to tell you will be entirely true; everything comes from books and from the Gospels… (*The* DRUNKARD *creeps up on the* ANGEL *again, and pulls out other feathers. He mimes admiring them. He fans himself and struts about. The* ANGEL *notices*) Drunkard!

DRUNKARD: Eh… ? (*Throwing the feathers in the air*) It's snowing!

ANGEL: Will you kindly leave the stage?!

DRUNKARD: I would quite willingly leave, if you would care to accompany me, because I am not capable of putting one foot in front of the other without falling down and banging my nose on the ground… If you would be so good as to accompany me, then I shall tell you about this beautiful drinking session I had…

ANGEL: I am not interested in your drinking session... Out! Out, or I shall kick you off the stage!

DRUNKARD: Ah? You'll kick me off?

ANGEL: Yes, I'll kick you off... Get out of here!

DRUNKARD: Kind people! Did you hear that? An angel who wants to kick me out... Me! An angel... (*Aggressively, turning to the* ANGEL) Come on, then, my big angel... Come and kick me off if you dare! Because I'll pull out all your feathers, like plucking a chicken! I shall pull out your feathers one by one, from your backside too... from your arse... Come on, my big chicken... Come on!

ANGEL: Help... Don't touch me! Help! Murderer... !

He flees.

DRUNKARD: Me, murderer? Did you hear that? He called me a murderer! I, who am so good that goodness pours out of my ears... and spills all over the floor, and you could almost slip on it... And how could I not be good, after that wonderful drinking session that I've been on? You know, I never imagined that today was going to end up so beautifully, because it began so wretchedly and miserably...

You see, I was invited to a wedding, a marriage, in a place near here, called Cana... Cana... In fact, in days to come they're going to talk of it: the Marriage at Cana. I was invited, as I say... I arrived, and there was all the whole table ready for the wedding feast, with all the food arranged on it... and nobody had sat down to eat yet. They were all standing up, and stamping around the place, and cursing.

There was the bride's mother. She was crying... There was the bride's father. He was banging his head against the wall, in a foul mood.

'But what's happened, what's happened?' I asked.

'Oh the shame of it...'

'Has the groom run off?'

'The groom is that fellow over there, swearing more than anyone.'

'Well, then, what's happened?'

'Oh the shame of it... We've just found out that an entire vat of wine, a barrel of wine that was prepared especially for the wedding banquet, has all turned to vinegar. We're in a right pickle!'

'Oh. Oh... All the wine turned to vinegar! How terrible! I've heard it said that a rained-on bride is supposed to be a lucky bride, but being rained on by vinegar would make her the kind of bad luck you'd want to keep away from...'

And everyone was crying and cursing, and the bride's mother was tearing her hair, and the bride was crying, and the bride's father was banging his head against the wall...

At that moment, a young fellow turned up, a certain Jesus, the one they've nicknamed... the 'Son of God'. And he wasn't alone, no! He was accompanied by his mother, whom they call the Madonna. A fine figure of a woman!!! They had been invited, and had turned up just a little late. Anyway, when this Mrs Madonna found out what a state everything was in, what with the wine being turned into vinegar and all, she went over to her son Jesus, son of God (and also of the Madonna) and said: 'You, my son, who are so good... you who do such wonderful things for everybody... see if you can manage to get these poor people out of the mess they're in.'

No sooner had the Madonna spoken to him, than all of a sudden everyone saw a sweet, sweet smile spread across Jesus' lips. His smile was so sweet that if you didn't watch out, it would make your kneecaps fall off and drop on your toes! What a sweet smile! When she finished talking, this young fellow gave his mother a kiss on the nose and said: 'Kind people, could I have twelve buckets full of good clean water?'

In a flash, twelve buckets arrived, full of water, and when I saw all that water all together at the same time, I felt a bit queasy. I felt like I was drowning, by heaven! Everyone fell silent, almost like being in church for the Sanctus, and this Jesus twirled his hands about a bit, snapping his fingers, and began to make signs over the water, the kind of signs that only sons of God make. I was standing a little bit away from the scene, because, as I said before, looking at water makes me nervous, and I wasn't even looking. I was just leaning to one side, all sad, and all of a sudden I caught a whiff in my nostrils of a smell that was unmistakably the aroma of crushed grapes...

You couldn't mistake it, it was wine! Heavens, what wine. They passed me a cup of it, and I put it to my lips and swallowed a drop. Heavens! Oh... Oh... Ye blessed in purgatory, what a wine! I had no sooner swallowed it when I got the taste; a bit bitter at the back, a bit sharp, almost spicy in the middle; it sent out a deep red sparkle, a glow, a wine without mould or froth, a wine of at least three years standing, a golden vintage! And it slips down your gullet, gurgles down to your stomach, spreads out a little, stays there for a bit, and then, wallop, comes rolling up again, up your gullet, in great waves, and the flavour hits your nostrils and spreads forth. A wine to stop a man in his tracks even if he were passing on a race-horse!

'It's spring,' he shouted. What a wine! And everyone began to clap Jesus 'Well done, Jesus! You're divine!' And the Madonna! The Madonna, his mother, was beside herself with happiness and pride at having a son who was so clever in bringing forth wine from water. Within a very short time we were all drunk. There was the bride's mother, dancing; the bride was in festive mood too; the bridegroom was leaping about; the bride's father was still in front of the wall, in a wicked mood, banging his head against it... because nobody had told him!

Jesus got up on a table, and began pouring wine for everybody: 'Drink, good people, be happy, get drunk, don't save it till later, enjoy yourselves... !'

And then, all of a sudden, he remembered his mother: 'Oh holy mother! Oh Madonna! Mother, I forgot, excuse me! Here, here's a drop for you too; drink a bit yourself.'

'No, no thank you, my son, thanks all the same, but I cannot drink, because I am not used to wine. It makes my head spin, and afterwards I start saying silly things.'

'But no, mother, it can't do you any harm. It will only make you a bit happy! This wine can't do you any harm; it's a pure wine, this, a good wine... I made it myself!'

And just imagine, there are still some damned rabble going around saying that wine is a creation of the devil, and that it's a sin, and that it's an invention of the most diabolical order. But do you think that if wine had really been an invention of the devil, that Jesus would have given some to his mother to drink? To his very own mother? Because Jesus had so much love for his mother that even I don't have for all the grappa in this world! I'm sure that if God the Father, in person, instead of leaving it so late when he taught Noah this wonderful trick of crushing the grape and bringing forth wine, if instead, right from the start, he had taught Adam, even before Eve, then we wouldn't be in this wretched state of a world that we are in now. We would all be in Paradise! Your health! Because on that wretched day when the wicked serpent came to visit Adam with the apple in his mouth, and told him: 'Eat the apple, Adam! It's sweet and good... Apples are sweet and red!!', then all it needed was for Adam to have a good big glass of wine near him, and... whoosh... he would have given a good kick to every apple on earth, and we would all be happy in Paradise!

That was the dreadful sin, because fruit was not created to be eaten, but to be trodden and crushed; because from crushed apples you make a good cider; from crushed cherries you make good sweet grappa; and as for the grape, it would be a mortal sin to eat it! Because with the grape, you make wine. And I am sure that those who have been good and honest in their lives... for them, Heaven is going to be made all of wine!

What do you mean, that's blasphemy? No, I am not blaspheming! You know, I dreamt once that I was dead. One night I had a dream that I had died, and I dreamt that they came to take me away. They took me to a terrible place, where there were a lot of deep basins, and inside each basin there stood one of the damned – poor souls! They were submerged, standing up in a great sea of red liquid, which looked like blood. And I immediately began to cry: 'Oh God! I am in Hell!' Miserable wretch, sinner that I was! And while I was weeping, they took all my clothes off, and began to wash me, rubbing me down and cleaning me to such an extent, with hot and cold water, that I have never been so clean in all my life, not even at Easter!

Once I was good and clean, they put me into one of those big basins, with its red liquid. Glug... glug... glug... And that red liquid rose up to my lips. I shut my mouth, but one of the ripples... splosh... came back at me... and went up my nose. Ooof! And I swallowed a great gulp. I was in Paradise... !!! It was wine, and immediately I realised that this wonderful invention had been created by God the Father, especially for the Blessed (because everyone there was Blessed) so that the blessed ones would not have to make too much effort, in the sense of having to lift up their glasses to drink every time, and then have to wait for them to be filled again. Instead, he took all the blessed ones, and immersed them all, right up to their ears, in huge glasses of wine, standing there, so that it came up to their lips, and all they had to do was open their mouths to say: 'Good morning, gentlemen,' and... glug... And I began to sing: 'My beloved is so fickle...' Glug... glug... Help... I'm drowning... Glug... What a lovely way to drown!!! Glug... Glug... Glug... Glug...

THE BIRTH OF THE JONGLEUR

Introduction

Here we have a picture (photo 12) of a drunkard, or rather a *jongleur* who is playing the part of a drunkard. This fresco dates back to around the year 1100. It comes from a little Romanesque church in Provence. It may be that he is acting precisely the piece that I've played tonight. At any rate, this piece appears in many languages and in different dialects. A version has been found even as far afield as Bavaria. The fact that *jongleurs* and their performances were even depicted on wall-paintings in churches reveals how important they were in their day.

I would now like to perform a new piece, which I have only played twice so far. Yesterday and the day before. I am still a bit nervous about doing it, because it is an extremely difficult piece to perform. It tells of the *Birth of the Jongleur*. The origins of this piece can be traced to Asia Minor, but the version that we know originates in Sicily. Sicily was linked to the East, not only by trade and commerce, but also by geographical and political factors, and thus by her culture. This was especially true in the 13th century, the period in which the piece which I am about to perform begins to be found in documented form.

There is another version in existence, which is rather older, although it is not possible to date it with precision. This version comes from my own part of the country (to be precise, from the area of Brescia-Cremona). The text as it was found was only a series of fragments. I had intended to reconstruct it, but I didn't have the courage to take it on. However, last year, I went to Sicily, and there, in the library at Ragusa, thanks to a comrade who took us there, we were able to find the entire text, in Sicilian dialect. Extraordinary! The piece is incredibly violent. I even went so far as to learn it in Sicilian. But since the language would sound rather archaic and incomprehensible to today's ears, I have translated it into Lombard dialect, which you will understand rather better.

Photo 12: 'The drunkard'. Twelfth-century fresco from Provence.

What does this piece relate? We see a *jongleur*, explaining how, before he became a *jongleur*, he was a peasant, and that it was Christ who changed him into a *jongleur*. How did it happen that Christ gave him this new profession? It was because he used to own land, but a landowner tried to take the land away from him. I say no more, because there's not really much that I can add. The piece speaks for itself. Don't worry if at first you don't understand some of what I say. The sense, the gestures and sounds involved will help you. By my gestures and by the sounds of the piece, you will easily grasp the meaning of this tale.

THE BIRTH OF THE JONGLEUR

Kind people, gather round and listen. The jongleur is here! I am the jongleur. I leap and pirouette, and make you laugh. I make fun of those in power, and I show you how puffed up and conceited are the bigshots who go around making wars in which *we* are the ones who get slaughtered. I reveal them for what they are. I pull out the plug, and... pssss... they deflate. Gather round, for now is the time and place that I begin to clown and teach you. I tumble, I sing and I joke! Look how my tongue whirls, almost like a knife. Remember that. But I have not always been... Well, I would like to tell you how it was that I came to be.

I was not born a jongleur; I didn't suddenly turn up as I am now, with a sudden gust from the skies and, hopla, there I was: 'Good day... Hello.' No! I am the result of a miracle! A miracle which was carried out on me. Do you believe me? This is how it came about! I was born a peasant.

A peasant? Yes, a real countryman. I was happy, I was sad, I had no land. No! I worked as all of us work in these valleys, wherever I could. And one day I came by a mountain, a mountain all of rock. It was nobody's. I found that out. I asked people. 'No! Nobody wants this mountain!'

Well, I went up to its peak, and I scratched with my nails, and I saw that there was a little bit of earth there, and I saw that there was a little trickle of water coming down. So I began to scratch further. I went down to the river bank, and I wore my fingers to the bone bringing earth up onto this mountain. And my children and my wife were there. My wife is sweet, sweet and fair, with two round breasts, and a gentle way of walking that reminds you of a heifer as she moves. Oh, she is beautiful! I love her, and it gives me such pleasure to speak of her.

Anyway, I carried earth up in my own hands, and the grass grew so fast! Pfff… ! It grew of its own accord. You've no idea how beautiful it was! It was like gold dust! I would stick in my hoe, and pfff… a tree sprang forth. That earth was a miracle! A marvel! There were poplars, oaks and other trees everywhere. I sowed them when the moon was right; I knew what had to be done, and there, sweet, fine, handsome crops grew. There was chicory, thistles, beans, turnips, there was everything. For me, for us!

Oh, how happy I was! We used to dance, and then it would rain for days on end, and then the sun would blaze, and I would come, and go, and the moons were always right, and there was never too much wind, or too much mist. It was beautiful, beautiful! It was our land. This set of terraces was really beautiful. Every day I built another one. It was like the tower of Babel, beautiful, with all these terraces. It was paradise, paradise on earth! I swear it. And all the peasants used to pass by, saying:

'That's amazing, look what you've managed to bring forth out of this pile of rocks! How stupid that I never thought of that!' And they were envious. One day the lord of the whole valley passed by. He took a look and said:

'Where did this tower spring up from? Whose is this land?'

'It's mine,' I said. 'I made it myself, with these hands. It was nobody's.'

'Nobody's? That "Nobody's" is a word that doesn't exist. It's mine!'

'No! It's not yours! I've even been to the lawyer, and he told me it was nobody's. I asked the priest, and he said it was nobody's. And I built it up, piece by piece.'

'It's mine, and you have to give it to me.'

'I cannot give it to you, sir. I cannot go and work for others.'

'I'll pay you for it; I'll give you money. Tell me how much you want.'

'No! No, I don't want money, because if you give me money, then I'll not be able to buy other land with the money that you give me, and I'll have to go and work for others again. No, I don't want to. I won't.'

'Give it to me.'

'No!'

Then he laughed, and went away. The next day the priest came, and he told me:

'The land belongs to the Lord of the Valley. Be sensible, give it up. Don't play the fool. Beware, because he is a powerful, evil lord. Give up this land. In the name of God, be sensible!'

'No!' I told him. 'I won't.'

And I made a rude gesture at him with my hand. Then the lawyer arrived too. He was sweating, by heaven, when he came up the mountain to find me.

'Be sensible. There are laws... and you should know that you can't... that, for you...'

'No! No!'

And I made a rude gesture at him too, and he went away, swearing.

But the lord didn't give up. No! He began by coming on hunting expeditions, and he sent all the hares chasing over my land. With his horses and his friends, he galloped to and fro across my land, breaking down my hedges. Then one day, he set fire to all my land. It was summer; a drought. He set fire to the whole of my mountain, and burned everything, even my animals and my house. But I wouldn't leave! I waited, and that night it began to rain. After the rain, I began to clear up, and put the fence posts back in position, and replace stones, and bring up fresh earth, and water everything. I was determined, by heaven, that I wouldn't move from there! And I did not move!

But one day he arrived, along with all his soldiers, and he was laughing. We were in the fields, my children, my wife and I. We were working. He arrived. He got down from his horse. He undid his breeches. He came over to my wife, grabbed her, threw her to the ground, ripped off her skirt and… I tried to move, but the soldiers held me fast. And he leapt upon her, and took her as if she were a cow. And I and the children had to stand there, with our eyes bursting from our heads, watching… I moved forward, with a leap. I managed to free myself. I took a hoe, and I shouted:

'You bastards!'

'Stop,' my wife cried. 'Don't do it. That's all they want, that's exactly what they are waiting for. If you raise your stick, then they will kill you. Don't you understand? They want to kill you and take away your land. That's all they want. He is bound to defend himself. It's not worth taking your stand against him. You have no honour to defend. You're poor, you're a peasant, a country person, you cannot go thinking of honour and dignity. That is stuff for rich people, for lords and nobles! They are entitled to get angry if people rape their wives and daughters. But you're not! Let it be. The land is worth more than your honour, or mine. It is worth more than everything! I have become a cow, a cow for the love of you.'

And I began to weep, weeping and looking all around. The children were weeping too. And the soldiers, with the lord of the valley, suddenly went off, laughing, happy and satisfied. We wept, how we wept! We could not even look each other in the eye. And when we went into the village, they began throwing rocks and stones at us. They shouted:

'Oh you ox, you who don't have the strength to defend your honour, because you have no honour. You are an animal. The lord has mounted your wife, and you stood there, without saying a word, for a handful of earth. You wretch!'

And when my wife went around the village:

'Whore, cow!' they shouted after her. And then they ran off. They would not even let her go into church. Nobody would let her! And the children couldn't go out in the village without everyone picking on them. And nobody would even look us in the eye. My wife ran off! I never saw her again; I don't know where she ended up. And my children wouldn't look at me. They fell ill, and wouldn't even cry. They died. I was left alone, alone, with this land. I didn't know what to do. One evening, I took a piece of rope, and threw it over a rafter.

I put the noose around my neck, and said to myself:

'Right. Now I am going to end it all, now!'

I was just about to do it, just about to hang myself, when I felt a hand on my shoulder. I turned round, and saw a fellow with big eyes and a pale face.

He says to me: 'Could you give me something to drink?'

'I ask you, in heaven's name, is this really the moment to come asking somebody for something to drink, when he's just about to hang himself?'

I look at him, and see that he too has the face of a poor wretch. Then I look further, and see that there are two more men, and they too have faces full of suffering.

'Alright, I'll give you something to drink. And *then* I'll hang myself.'

So I go to get them something to drink, and I take a good look at them:

'Instead of something to drink, you people look as if you could do with something to eat! It's been days and days since I last cooked anything to eat... But anyway, if you want, there is food.'

I took a pan and put it on the fire to heat up some broad beans. I gave them some, one bowl apiece, and how they ate! I, personally, wasn't very hungry. 'I'll wait till they've finished eating,' I thought, 'and then I'll hang myself.' Anyway, while they were eating, the one with the biggest eyes, who looked like a right poor devil, began to smile. He said:

'That's a terrible story, that you're going to hang yourself. I know why you want to do it, though. You have lost everything, your wife, your children, and all you are left with is your land. Yes, I know how it is! But if I were you, I wouldn't do it.'

And he carried on eating. How he ate! Then, in the end, he laid aside the utensils, and said:

'Do you know who I am?'

'No, but I've got an idea that you might be Jesus Christ.'

'Well done! You've guessed correctly. And this is St Peter, and that over there is St Mark.'

'Pleased to meet you! And what are you doing in these parts?'

'My friend, you've given me something to eat, and now I'm going to give you something to say.'

'Something to say? What is this "something"?'

'You poor fellow! It's right that you have held onto your land; it is right that you don't want bosses over you; it is right that you have had the strength not to give in; it's right... I like you. You're a good man, a strong man. But you're missing something which is also right, and which you should have: here and here. (*He points to his forehead and to his mouth*) You shouldn't remain here stuck to your land. You should move around the country, and when people throw stones at you, you should tell them, and help them to understand, and deflate that great bladder of a landlord. You should deflate him with the sharpness of your tongue, and drain him of all his poison and his stinking bile. You must crush these nobles, these priests, and all those who surround them: notaries, lawyers, etc. Not only for your own good, for your own land, but also for those like yourself who don't have land, who have nothing, and whose only right is the right to suffer, and who have no dignity to boast of. Teach them to survive with their brains, not just with their hands!'

'But don't you understand? I am not able. I have a tongue which refuses to budge. I stumble over every word. I have no education, and my brain is weak and useless. How am I supposed to do the things you suggest, and go about speaking to other people?'

'Don't worry. You will now see a miracle.'

He took my head in his hands, and drew me to him. Then he said:

'I am Jesus Christ. I have come to give you the power of speech. And this tongue of yours will lash, and will slash like a sword, deflating inflated balloons all over the land. You will speak out against bosses, and crush them, so that others can understand and learn, so that others can laugh at them and make fun of them, because it is only with laughter that the bosses will be destroyed. When you laugh at the rulers, the ruler goes from being a mountain, to being a little molehill, and then a nothingness. Here, I shall give you a kiss, and that will enable you to speak.'

He kissed me on the mouth. He kissed me for a long time. And suddenly I felt my tongue dart about inside my head, and my brain began to move, and my legs began to move with a mind of their own, and I went out in the streets of the village, and began to shout:

'Gather round, people! Gather round! hear ye! The *jongleur* is here! I am going to play a satire for you. I am going to joust with the lord of the land, for he is a great balloon, and I am going to burst him with the sharpness of my tongue. I shall tell you everything, how things come and go, and how it is not God who steals! It is those who steal and go unpunished... it is those who make big books of laws... *They* are the ones... And we must speak out, speak out. Listen, people – these rulers must be broken, they must be crushed...!

Photo 13: 'The birth of the villeyn', from a fourteenth-century manuscript.

THE BIRTH OF THE VILLEYN

Introduction

Here we have a picture (photo 13) taken from a miniature. It shows a piece being acted out by a famous *jongleur*, Matazone da Caligano. Matazone is a nickname which means 'cheerful fellow' (as you see, *jongleurs'* nicknames are not always rude – there are exceptions). Caligano, or Carignano, is a village near Pavia. The local dialect, a dialect of what was then the territory of Pavia, is very easy for us Lombards to understand. And, in fact, I played this piece in Sicily one time, and everybody was able to understand it. Anyway, as you can see, up there we have an angel; here is the landowner, the lord, the lord of the land... and here we have the peasant, or, rather, the villeyn.

What's going on in this picture? It depicts the moment when the landowner is being presented with the first villeyn ever to have been created by the Holy Father. The story of this piece is as follows: After seven times seven generations of working the land, Man goes to the Holy Father and says: 'Listen, I can't stand it any longer. I'm working too hard. You must relieve me of some of my work. You promised me that you were going to make things a bit easier for me!' 'What do you mean?!' says the Holy Father. 'I gave you a donkey, a mule, a horse, an ox, to make life easier for you.' 'Yes, true, but it's still me who has to push behind the plough,' said Man. 'And it's still me who has to go and muck out the cowsheds, and it's still me who has to do all the lowliest jobs, like spreading dung on the fields, milking, killing the pig... I want you to create me someone who can help me in all this, in fact someone who can take my place, so that I can finally get some rest!' 'Ah, so it's a villeyn that you want!' 'What's a villeyn?' 'It's exactly what you're looking for... But obviously, you wouldn't know that, because I haven't created him yet! Come on, let's go and create him now...' So, they go to see Adam. No sooner does Adam see the Eternal Father arriving together with another man than, hopla, he wraps his arms round his ribs, and shouts: 'No, not again! I'm not giving up another single rib!'

'Well, I suppose you're right too,' says the Eternal Father. 'But what am I supposed to do?' At that moment, a donkey passes by, and the Eternal Father has an idea: he waves his hand, and the donkey begins to swell up. It's pregnant.

Right: from this point I shall follow the original text. Here we have the words of Matazone da Caligano. A printed text exists, slightly different from the one which I am about to perform, which has been reconstructed by putting together various fragments, in order to give greater continuity and logic to the piece.

THE BIRTH OF THE VILLEYN

The story goes, in an old book long since forgotten, that with the passing of seven times seven generations from the sad day of his expulsion from Paradise, Man was fed up and beside himself with the amount of work that he had to do in order to survive. He went to see God, personally. He began weeping, and begged him to send someone to give him a hand to do the work on his land, because he could no longer manage it on his own. 'But don't you have donkeys and oxen for that?' God replied. 'You are right, Lord God, but it is always we men who have to stand behind the plough and push it like wretches, and the asses aren't capable of pruning vines, and no matter how carefully we teach them, they haven't yet learnt to milk cows. All this labour is making us old before our time, and our women are fading away... They're worn out by the time they reach twenty.'

God, who is so good to all, when he heard these things, was seized with compassion. He sighed, saying: 'Well, I am going to create for you a two-legged creature who will come and relieve you of this suffering'. He went straight away to Adam: 'Listen, Adam, I come to ask you a favour: lift up your shirt, because I need to take another of your ribs, to use it for an experiment.'

But when Adam heard this, he began to weep: 'Lord, have pity on me, because you have already taken one rib in order to create my wife, the treacherous Eve... If you take yet another rib, I won't have enough left to keep my stomach in, and all my innards will fall out like a gutted chicken.'

'You're right too,' God murmured, scratching his head. 'What am I supposed to do?'

At that moment, a donkey was passing, and God had a sudden idea; when it comes to ideas, God is a veritable volcano! He waved his hand at the ass, and the ass promptly swelled up. After nine months, the beast's belly was swollen to bursting point... Suddenly a loud noise was heard. The ass let out an enormous fart, and at that point out leapt the villeyn, all stinking.

(*Aside*) 'Oh, what a lovely nativity!'

(*Aside*) 'Shut up, you!'

At that moment, a tremendous storm broke, and the rains flooded down, washing over the ass's offspring. Then followed hail and a blizzard and thunder and lightning and all kinds of things, battering the villeyn's body, so that he would be in no doubt about the kind of life that was in store for him. As soon as he was properly clean, the Angel of the Lord came down and called to Man, saying:

'By order of God, you, from this moment, will be the boss, the greater one, and he, the villeyn, the lesser one. Now it is written and laid down that this villeyn shall live on coarse bread and raw onions, broad beans and boiled beans and spittle.

'He is to sleep on a straw pallet, so that he always remembers his status. Since he has been born naked, give him a bit of rough canvas, the kind they use for holding fish, so that he can make himself a nice pair of trousers. Breeches, which must have an opening down the middle, and with no laces, so that he doesn't waste too much time when he pisses.'

We could almost be dealing with today's employers, here!
As I go round Italy doing these shows, I often find myself
brought up against these cruder facts of life. For example, we
were performing in Verona one time, and some girls turned
up in the theatre, with posters that they hung around the
walls. They were on strike. They were on strike because their
employer had banned them from going to the toilet. In other
words, one of them felt the need... 'Excuse me, may I...?'
'No... No!' They were all supposed to go to the toilet at 11.25
sharp: the bell rings, and you do a wee. And anybody who
doesn't feel the need at that precise moment, too bad; they
have to wait till the next time.

These women were on strike in order to obtain the
privilege of doing a wee when they felt the urge. I don't know
how the story finished up... but maybe the most grotesque
incident was at the Ducati plant in Bologna, a very large
factory, world-scale – a major plant, in short. So, what
happened there? The bosses of this particular factory decided
to cut down the time allowed to workers for going to the
toilet. Some people would stay in there for four minutes,
some for as long as seven minutes, and the employers had had
enough! They argued with the trade unions, and there was a
tremendous struggle, and after a while they decided: 'Two
minutes and thirty five seconds are more than sufficient for a
person to fulfil their bodily needs...' Now, put like that it
sounds almost reasonable. A person would think: 'Well, they
must have carried out studies, they must have consulted
technicians and experts etc.' But I can assure you, believe me,
to do it in that time would be a record!

Two minutes and thirty-five seconds: a record! And these
days, the Ducati workers don't just go to the toilet... they go
into training at home first. If you don't believe that this is a
record, try it for yourself. Take a couple of interesting
books, wait for a good day, put on a nice record of soothing
Hawaiian music (it's very helpful in this connection...) and, as
you will see, IT CAN'T BE DONE! And it particularly can't
be done when you're neurotic about clocks that go tick-tock,
tick-tock. Yes! Because in every toilet at the Ducati factory
there is a timing mechanism! As soon as you go in, it starts,

tick-tock, tick-tock. But the truly grotesque part of the situation is still to come. How do you know when your time has run out? Obviously, you would imagine that the worker goes into the toilet cubicle (*He mimes going into a toilet*) and tick-tock, tick-tock... he takes a deep breath... (*He takes a deep breath*) ...like when you're about to dive into a cold swimming pool... and then (*He mimes*) tick-tock... tick-tock... PEEEEEP! (*A whistle*).

Now, it's logical that if the gadget is going to go off, it means that there must be a button under the toilet seat. No? That way, when you sit on the seat, it pushes down the button and sets off the timing mechanism. But the employer knows that the worker is pretty smart. Given half a chance, he'll try to avoid actually sitting on the seat, and will balance on his toes, poised over the pan, so that he can stay in the cubicle for hours on end. 'Ah!' says the employer. 'Now I'm going to fix you.' So, the push-button is not fixed under the toilet seat at all, but works off the door-handle! In other words, as soon as the worker puts his hand on the door-handle, the electric switch trips, and it begins. Tick-tock... tick-tock. 'Damn these braces, I can't... Hell and damnation... The paper...' (*A whistle. Then, looking down into the pan*) 'Pardon the intrusion.'

So, you have to get into training. You have to arrive with your bowels well loosened and ready for action... The first thing to remember is that you should arrive without your trousers on. You should have your trousers already folded, on your shoulder... Actually, this can look quite stylish... like a sort of scarf... Your shirt should be tucked up, like a native dancing girl (*All this is mimed*) because otherwise it'll get in the way. And above all, don't suddenly stop and think: 'Oh God...' (*He tries to cover himself in front with his hands*) You must forget all that silly stuff about nudity being embarrassing.

A German academic by name of Otto Weininger has made some extraordinary studies of this question: this man discovered that it is only when you adopt an attitude of shame that others become aware of the fact that you are naked. It's logical. If you go around like this (*He mimes a person covering his genitals and his backside with his hands*), people will immediately point at you: 'Ooh! A naked man!! Look, Mummy, a naked man!' But if you free yourself of this idiotic sense of shame, and just relax, then who's going to worry? There you are, stark naked, happy, relaxed, walking down the street, and people will say: 'Oh, look, a duke!'

So there you are, the worker must become a duke when he goes to the toilet; and, in addition to learning how to match the speed of the assembly line, he must also learn to handle the time limits set by the toilet cubicle. These two aspects of time and motion are different, but fundamental. (*He mimes a worker going into a toilet cubicle and sitting down*) One… two… three… A dance!

Anyway, let's get back to the story of the villeyn. The angel hands the villeyn over to his new employer. Let's listen to the angel's advice to the employer, regarding how to treat the man.*

THE BIRTH OF THE VILLEYN

As his coat of arms
Give him a pick and shovel over his shoulder.
Ensure that he goes round barefoot all the time,
For he will not complain.
In January give him a pitchfork over his shoulder
And send him to muck out the cowsheds.
In February send him to sweat in the fields, breaking the
     soil.
Don't worry if he gets sores round his neck,
If he's full of cuts and callouses,
Because your horse will benefit from it,
No longer will it be troubled by midges and dung flies
Because the flies will all go and live in the villeyn's house.
Tax everything that he does,
Tax him even when he shits.
At carnival time allow him to dance,
And even sing, let him enjoy himself,
But not too much, because he must not forget
That he exists in this world in order to labour.

Translator's note: In the original, line endings rhymed.

In March too make him go barefoot.
Let him prune your vine when it has rust.
In the month of April
He should stay in the sheep-pen,
Sleeping with the sheep,
And let him sleep with open eyes,
Because the wolf is hungry!
If the hungry wolf is looking for something to eat,
Then let him take the villeyn, for I shall not complain.
In May, send him to cut the violet-strewn grass
But make sure that he does not get distracted,
Running after pretty girls.
And as for the girls, they are pretty and buxom.
What matter if they are peasants,
Bring them, to play and dance with you for the whole
    month.
Then, when you tire of them,
Give them to the villeyn to marry,
Give them in marriage already pregnant,
Which will save them from having to work.
In June, you must send the villeyn
To pick cherries from the trees,
As well as plums and peaches and apricots,
But first, so that he doesn't eat all the best ones,
Make him eat dry bread, which will block up his bowels.
In July and August,
When the burning heat is on us,
Slake his thirst.
Give him vinegar to drink
And if he gets angry and swears,
Do not worry that he has sinned:
Because the peasant, be he good or evil,
Is anyway destined to Hell.
In the month of September,
Let him relax,
Send him to harvest the grapes.
But make sure that he works hard at the wine-treading,
So that he is too tired to go and get drunk.
In fine October, have him kill the pig,

And as a reward let him have its entrails,
But not all of them,
Because some are good for making skins for sausages.
Leave the villeyn with blood-sausages,
Which are poisonous and noxious.
Your good, solid hams
You should leave in the hands of your villeyns –
Leave them the hams to salt.
Then have them bring them
To your house, which will give you a handsome feed.
In November, and then in December,
Make sure that the cold does not harm him,
Keep your peasant warm –
Send him to cut wood,
And make sure that he goes back again and again,
And that each time he comes well-loaded,
Because in this way he will not catch cold.
And when he comes near to the fire,
Send him packing,
Send him out of doors,
Because a fire will only make him soft.
If it is pouring with rain outside,
Tell him to go to Mass,
Because in church he will find shelter,
And he can pray,
Pass his time praying,
Because anyway it won't do him any good.
Because, anyway, he won't win salvation,
Because the peasant doesn't have a soul,
And God cannot listen to him.
And how could a stupid peasant hope to have a soul,
Given that he was born from an ass, blown out by a fart?

I would like to pause for a moment on one detail of this story:
the question of the soul. As Matazone says: 'You, villeyn, you
cannot have a soul, because you were born of an ass.' Well,
this is virtually telling him to accept his condition, to not
accept the soul, inasmuch as the soul provides a pretext for

one of the greatest blackmails ever perpetrated against mankind. We find this sentiment in Bonvesin de la Riva, in his *Dialogue Between the Soul and the Body*: 'Thank the Lord, Soul, that you do not have a backside, because, if you did, I would give it a good kicking: you are like lead to me; I cannot fly, because you weigh me down.'

Now, why this rejection of the soul? Because it is one of the greatest blackmails that the bosses can use against us. In a moment of desperation, one might come to the point of saying: 'So what do I care, let's have at least a minimum of dignity. I am going to stab that bastard boss of mine!' So then the boss, or rather the boss through the medium of the priest, comes along and says: 'No! Stop! Do you want to ruin yourself? You have suffered all your life, and now, shortly, you are going to die. You have the possibility of going to heaven now, because Jesus Christ told you that since you are the last among men you shall enter into the kingdom of heaven... And now you want to ruin everything? Think what you're doing, don't get rebellious! And wait for the after-life. I, for my part, am damned! I, for my misfortunes, am a boss. And what did Jesus Christ say about me? He said: "You will never enter into the kingdom of heaven. You are like the camel which will never pass through the eye of a needle." You see the con? Obviously, I, as employer, have to make my own little Paradise here on earth, and it's for that reason that I keep you down and rob you and grind you down. To be sure, I even rob you of your soul, it's true! I want my little Paradise here and now; it may be small, but I want it all for myself; and I want it for all the time that I am here on earth. You are lucky, though! You will have everything. You will have Paradise! You will only get it after death, it's true, but you will have it for all Eternity!'

THE RESURRECTION OF LAZARUS

Introduction

Now let us move on to the miracle of the Resurrection of Lazarus.

This piece was regarded as the *pièce de resistance* among virtuoso *jongleurs*, because in it the *jongleur* has to act out something like 15 different characters in succession, and only indicates the character changes with his body. He does not vary his voice at all; everything is done by gesture. This kind of piece requires the performer to play it a bit by ear, according to the responses of laughter, silence, etc that he gets from the audience. In effect, it is a basic framework which then gives a possibility for improvisation. The principle theme of this piece is a satirisation of everything that passes for the 'moment of mystery'. This is achieved by playing out an event which, among the people, passes for a 'miracle'. The satire is aimed at the miracle-mongers, the magicians, the conjurors' art of the miraculous, which is an underlying feature of many religions, including Catholicism. The piece deals with the way in which miracles are presented as supernatural happenings, which must have been performed by God. At the origins of these miracle stories, the principal notion is that of God's love and sympathy for the people, for mankind.

Here, though, the story of the miracle is told from the standpoint of the people. The scene is set as if it were a show about to be performed by a great conjuror, a magician, somebody who is able to do extraordinary and vastly entertaining things. Here there is no hint of the religious content which is supposed to lie behind the miracle.

In a cartoon wall-painting in Pisa cemetery, there is a portrayal of the Resurrection of Lazarus. (A cartoon is the original sketch which precedes the final stage of a fresco; in this case the fresco had been removed for restoration, and the well-preserved cartoon was revealed). Lazarus does not even

Photo 14: 'The resurrection of Lazarus', drawing by Dario Fo, based on a fresco in Pisa cemetery.

figure in the scene. One's attention is concentrated wholly on the crowd, on the people – almost like a theatre audience – struck with amazement. Their gestures express their marvel at the miracle under way. Within the picture, which is itself grotesque (almost as if theatre and figurative representation were going hand in hand) there is an added element of the grotesque. We find one of the characters (photo 14) dipping his fingers into the purse of a spectator standing near him. He is taking advantage of the miracle, of people's amazement and sense of wonderment, in order to steal their money!

THE RESURRECTION OF LAZARUS

'Excuse me. Is this the graveyard, the cemetery where they're going to perform the Resurrection of Lazarus?'

'Yes, this is the one.'

'Ah, good.'

'One moment… That'll be ten pence, to get in.'

'Ten pence?'

'Well, alright, let's make it two.'

'Tuppence?! Why, in hell's name?!'

'Because I am the guardian of the cemetery, and all you people coming in here are going to wreck the place. You'll ruin my hedges and trample my grass, and I must be recompensed for all the trouble and damage that you're going to cause. Two pence, or you won't see the miracle.'

'Alright! You don't miss a chance, do you! There you go!'

'Two pence for you others as well. And I don't care if you've got children… I don't care. They're here for the show too, aren't they? Well, alright… half a penny. Hey, you, wretch! Down off that wall! Cunning devil, he wants to see the miracle for free! He should pay, no? Two pence… No, no, you did *not* pay before. That'll be two pence for you too, tuppence to get in…'

'Pretty crafty that one, making money out of miracles. Anyway, now I'll have to find where Lazarus is. His name must be on his tomb! The last time I came to see a miracle here, I spent half a day waiting around, and then they ended up doing the miracle right over the back there! And I had to stand here like an idiot watching from a distance. But this time I've taken the trouble to find out the fellow's name in advance, and I'm going to look for it on the tomb. I'll be in the front row this time! Lazarus… (*Hunting around*) And I'll put myself… Lazarus… I'll put myself right next to the tomb, and that way I'll see everything… Lazarus… But then even if I do find the tomb with Lazarus written on it, I can't read, so I won't know, will I! Still, I suppose I'll just have to guess. I'll stand here. I didn't do so well last time, but let's hope it goes better this time.'

'Who's that pushing? No, don't start pushing! I got here first, and I'm having the front position! I don't care if you are only little! Little people should come first thing in the morning and reserve themselves a position. Pretty clever, eh? He's little, so he wants to get in front! Supposing we were to stand in order of height? The little ones in front, and the big ones behind! Then the little ones would all turn up afterwards, and it would be as if they'd got here first! Stop pushing, you're going to push me into the tomb! For heaven's sake! I don't care. Get back. Eh? Oh! Now the women are pushing as well!'

'Hasn't he arrived yet? Isn't it time for the miracle?'

'Isn't there someone here who knows this Jesus Christ, who could go and get him to hurry up, because we're all here, waiting? After all, you can't wait for miracles for ever, eh?! They should set a timetable and stick to it!'

'Chairs! Who wants chairs! Chairs for hire, ladies! Two pence per chair! Make sure that you've got a seat, ladies, because when the miracle happens and the Holy Man brings Lazarus back to life, and he starts talking, and singing, and moving around, then you'll get a fright; you'll see his eyes glistening and gleaming, and you'll faint. You'll finish up falling backwards and banging your heads on a rock, and you'll end up dead! Dead! And this Holy Man only does one miracle per day! Chairs for hire! Only two pence!'

'I see, you only think about making money, do you, eh?'

'So, doesn't anybody want to…?'

'Don't push! I don't care…!'

'Stop climbing up on the chairs! Ah, pretty clever! Do you see that? The little fellow has climbed up on a chair now!'

'And don't lean on me, because I'm right on the edge of the grave, and…'

'Is he coming? Hasn't he arrived yet?'

'Sardines! Tasty sardines! Tuppence a time! Very tasty! Freshly grilled! Lovely sardines! Sardines to raise the dead! Two pence!'

(*Calling him over*) 'Sardines… give a couple to Lazarus, to prepare his stomach!'

'Shut up, blasphemer!'

'Behave yourselves.'

'He's coming! He's coming! Here he is!'

'Who is? Where?'

'Jesus!'

'Which one is he?'

'The dark one? Ugh! He looks pretty mean!'

'No! That's Mark!'

'Is Jesus the one behind?'

'Which one, the tall one?'

'No, the little one.'

'The lad?'

'Yes, the one over there with the little beard.'

'Oh, but he's only a young lad, for goodness sake.'

'Look! The whole lot of them are with him.'

'Oh, look, there's John! I know that John... (*Calling to him*) John! Jesus! What a nice fellow that Jesus is!'

'Oh! Look! The Madonna's there too! There's his whole family. But does he always go round with all these people? Hey...!'

'Well, they won't let him go around on his own, on account that he's a bit crazy!'

(*Calling to him*) 'Jesus?! What a nice fellow. He winked at me.'

'Jesus! Jesus! Do us the miracle of the loaves and the fishes like you did last time. They were really good!'

'Shut up! Blasphemer, behave yourself!'

'Silence! Get down on your knees. He's made a sign for everyone to go down on their knees, because we have to pray.'

'Where's the tomb?'

'Eh...? It's that one over there.'

'Oh, look! He's told them to lift off the tomb cover.'

'Ooooh... !'

'Shut up!'

'On your knees, on your knees. Come on, everyone down on your knees!'

'No, not me! I'm not going down on my knees, because I don't believe, I'm not a believer.'

'Oh, look at that!'

'Shut up!'

'Let me see.'

'No! Get down from there, down off that chair.'

'No! Let me get up there, because I want to see!'

'For goodness sake! Look! They've lifted the tombstone, and there's the corpse inside. There he is, it's Lazarus, and what a stink! What is that vile smell?'

'Good heavens!'

'What is it?'

'Shut up!'

'Let me look!'

'He's full of worms, and what a stink! Goodness! He must have been dead for at least a month, and he's all coming apart. Oh, what a rotten corpse they've landed him with! What a lousy trick! I'm sure he's not going to be able to manage it this time, poor devil!'

'There's no way he can do it, never! Impossible for anyone to bring *that* back to life. He's all gone rotten! What a joke! Lousy bums! They told him that the man had only been dead for three days! It must be a month at least! What a sight! Poor Jesus!'

'I say he can still do it, though! This man is a holy man, and he can do the miracle even when the body has been rotting for a month!'

'I say that he can't do it!'

'Do you want to bet?'

'OK, let's have a bet!'

'Right! Two pence! Three pence! Ten pence! What do you want to bet?'

'Shall I keep the money? Trust me! Here we all trust each other, don't we? Alright, I'll look after the money!'

'Behave yourselves! Now, pay attention! Everyone on your knees, and silence!'

'What's he doing?'

'He's beginning to pray.'

'Quiet, eh!'

'Hey there, Lazarus, rise up!'

'Ha, ha, you might as well tell him to come out and sing as well, because the only things that are going to come out are the worms that are in him! Rise up, indeed!?'

'Quiet! Look, he's risen up onto one knee!'

'Who? Jesus?'

'No! Lazarus! Heavens, look!'

'Nooo… ! It's impossible!'

'Let me see.'

'Oh, look! He's moving, he's moving, he's on his feet, come on! Oh, he's fallen! Now he's moving again, he's on his feet.'

'A miracle! Oh, a miracle. Oh Jesus, sweet creature that you are, and to think that I didn't believe in you!'

'Well done, Jesus!'

'I've won the bet. Let's have the money. Hey, don't mess about…'

'Well done, Jesus!'

'My purse! They've stolen my purse! Stop, thief!'

'Jesus, well done!'

'Stop, thief!'

'Well done, Jesus! Well done, Jesus…!'

'Stop, thief!'

BONIFACE VIII

Introduction

And now we come to Boniface VIII. Boniface was Pope in the days of Dante Alighieri. Dante was well acquainted with the man: his hatred of him was such that he consigned him to Hell in his *Inferno* even before he was dead. Somebody else who hated him, albeit a little differently, was the Franciscan monk, Jacopone da Todi, an active and militant member of the Poor Brotherhood; in other words, in today's parlance, an extremist. He was tied up with the movement of poor peasants, particularly in the region where he lived. In breach of one of the laws enacted by Boniface VIII (who, by the way, was a crook of the first order), Jacopone had uttered the following verse: *Ah! Bonifax, che come putta hai tràito la Ecclesia*. In other words, 'Boniface, you who have reduced the Church to a whore!'

Boniface, obviously, was very taken with Jacopone: when he finally managed to get his hands on the monk (who, incidentally, was an extraordinary man of the theatre), he threw him into jail, and forced him to remain seated, in this position (*He demonstrates*), with his arms spread and his feet tied, for five long years. Chained in his own excrement. And they say that after five years, when Jacopone was finally released from prison after the death of this Boniface, the poor friar, even though still a young man, was no longer even able to walk: he was literally bent double, and that's how he got around. Then, a year and a half later, he died. They tried to stretch him out in his coffin, but it proved impossible. Every time they stretched him out... Creeeak... he simply folded up as before. In the end, they had enough, and buried him sitting upright!

However, he wasn't the only one with an abiding hatred of the Papacy. Gioacchino da Fiore, who lived well before the times of St Francis (who was more or less the father of all heretical movements within the church), argued along the following lines:

'If we want to bring dignity to the church of Christ, we must destroy the Church. The great beast of Rome, the mighty monster of Rome. And in order to destroy the Church, it is not enough for us to bring down the walls, the roofs and the belfries; we must also destroy those who rule it: the Pope, the bishops and the cardinals.'

A fairly radical point of view!

Anyway, the Pope of that period immediately sent a hundred or so armed troops to visit him. They went looking for him on the mountain where he lived, and thanks to an informer they found his cave. But, unfortunately for them, they arrived only to find him dead; still warm, but dead nonetheless. He had died two minutes before they arrived. We don't know whether he died from fright at seeing the soldiers arriving, or just because he was a bit mischievous and wanted to upset them. I suspect it was the latter: Gioacchino da Fiore had a wicked sense of humour.

Here we have an extremely realistic portrayal (photo 15) of Boniface VIII. We see him using the monk Segalello da Parma as a chair to sit on. Segalello of Parma was a member of the 'Sackcloth' order of monks, so called because they dressed in sackcloth. Another extremist, in the language of today's newspapers...

So, this particular extremist, whom we see here providing a seat for the Pope, was one of those who demanded that the Pope and Church should be poor, extremely poor, and that all their wealth should be handed over to the poor of the world. In Segalello's words: 'The dignity of the Church should be founded on the dignity of the poor.'

In other words, when the Church has within it a large body of people who are dying of hunger, then that Church has very little to be proud of. Incidentally, this fellow had an interesting nickname. The local people called him Segarello – little wanker. Segalello was a member of an order that preached absolute chastity, and he obviously got his nickname from the

Photo 15: 'Boniface VIII'. Reconstruction from a
    fourteenth-century codex.

fact that nobody ever saw him go with women. Anyway, this monk with his jester's nickname used to go round stirring up the peasantry:

'Good morning, my friends, what are you up to? Enjoying yourselves? No? You're digging the earth? You're work-ing! And whose is this land? Yours, I presume! No? It's not yours? How can that be! You work the land and... But you must gain the profits from it?! What profits? Ah... you take such a low percentage? And what's that you say? The owner keeps the rest for himself? The owner of what?! Of the earth? Ha, ha, ha! The earth has an owner? Do you really believe that in the Bible the land was handed over to people so that they could own it...? Fools! Imbeciles! The land is yours; they took it for themselves, and then they gave it to you to work. The land who belongs to those who work it, don't you see?!'

Just imagine, in the Middle Ages, going round saying things like that: the land belongs to those who work it! You'd have to be raving mad to go round saying it even nowadays... so just imagine, in the Middle Ages! Anyway, they promptly arrested him and burned him at the stake, himself and his whole brotherhood of 'Sackcloth' Friars.

Only one got away. He was known as Fra' Dolcino, and he went off back to where he used to live, near Vercelli. But despite his narrow escape, far from staying quietly at home, he too decided to go round stirring up the peasantry. He took to the streets as a jester. He would go up to people and start:

'Hey, peasant! The land is yours. Take it! Fool, imbecile, the land belongs to those who work it...'

And the peasants of the Vercelli countryside (perhaps because he spoke their local dialect and they could understand him) looked at him and said: 'Hey... That Fra' Dolcino is a bit crazy! But what he says is pretty sensible! You know what, I've got a mind to keep this land for myself... No. Why don't we leave the land to the landowner, and instead I'll just keep the harvest.' So, from that day on, every time the landowners' henchmen arrived, the peasants used to stone them. And the peasants began to tear up their contract, which in those days was called the *angheria* – in other words, 'oppression'. That's right, the contract which existed between peasants and the landowners in the Middle Ages was called 'oppression'. Of course, in those days it only meant 'contract'; but anyway, the people soon began to see the true nature of this contract, and the word took on other meanings: the word that used to mean contract between peasant and landowner came to be synonymous with oppression.

So, the peasants were beginning to tear up this contract. But they realised that they could not hope to win on their own. So they began to organise together and unite all the peasants in the region. In addition, realising that in order to build their strength they would have to extend their organisation, they began setting up links with the waged workers – in other words, the small artisans – who were beginning to develop in large numbers in the Middle Ages. This led to the organisation of an extraordinary community: they called themselves the 'communards' (*comunitardi*).

These were the first commune-dwellers in our history; their organisation was built around the *credenza*, in other words, the food cupboard. In Italy, from north to south, the word *credenza* means the pantry, the place where we keep food in the house. This noun obviously derives from the verb *credere* ('to believe'), to believe in something. So, *credenza*, the food cupboard, from *credere*, to believe, to believe in the community. These forms of communes had already begun to exist in the 6th century AD. The first *credenza* which comes down to us through history is the *credenza* of the commune of Sant'Ambrogio; an enormous, giant food cupboard, with little doors and separate storage spaces in which the commune's food could be kept, in order to protect grain from the damp, and to feed the commune in periods of famine.

However, expectation of famine was not a major consideration in the distribution of the common wealth; everyone would gather, and the food was distributed to each according to their needs. Bear that in mind – to each according to their needs; not according to the work that each had put in.

This method of self-government was beginning to upset the landowners – particularly those who felt that they had been 'robbed' of their land. One in particular, the Count of Monferrato, organised a punitive expedition. Setting off with a gang of his henchmen, he managed to capture a hundred or so communards. He cut off their hands and feet. This was a style of the times. In Brittany, two hundred years previously, the nobles had done the same with their own peasantry. Anyway, minus their hands and feet, they were mounted on donkeys and driven to the city of Vercelli. This, in order that the communards should realise what happened to people who took too many liberties.

When the communards saw their own brothers in this sorry mutilated state, they did not sit down and weep. That same night they set off, and unexpectedly marched into Novara. They entered the city, and carried out a full-scale massacre of the Count's murderous thugs and assassins. In addition, they succeeded in convincing the local population to seek their freedom, and organise themselves too into a commune. The movement spread with incredible rapidity. Oleggio, Pombia, Castelletto Ticino, Arona, the whole northern area of Lago Maggiore, Domodossola, the area by Monte Rosa, the whole of Lago d'Otra, Valsesia, Varallo, Val Mastallone, Ivrea, Biella, Alessandria... In short, half of Lombardy and half of Piedmont was in a state of rebellion. The local nobility, the dukes and counts, did not know what to do. They sent an envoy to Rome, who went to see the Pope, shouting: 'Help, help, you must help us, in the name of God!'

Well, faced with this 'in the name of God', what was the Pope to do? 'Forsooth, in the name of God, I must help them...' Luckily for him – and luckily for the northern nobility – the Fourth Crusade was about to embark from Brindisi (this, by the way, is the Crusade about which we know nothing, because nothing is ever written about it, and you usually find that what is passed off as the 'Fourth' Crusade was in fact the Fifth). The Pope sent his envoy with a message for the crusaders: 'Stop, everybody. Sorry, I made a mistake. The infidels are not on the other side of the ocean – they're up north, in Lombardy, in the guise of rebellious peasants. Off you go, at once!'

So, after a long march, eight thousand men (almost all of them Germans) arrived in Lombardy. They joined up with troops of the noble families of Visconti, Modrone, Torriani, Borromeo and the Count of Monferrato – along with the Savoys, another noble family which was beginning to get under way in that period. The net result was a vicious massacre. They succeeded in cutting off three thousand communards on a mountain near Biella. Men, women and children. At one fell swoop, they slaughtered the lot of them, burned them, and slit their throats...

Needless to say, this history which I have briefly summarised for you, receives no mention in the history books used in our schools. This of course is quite natural. After all, who organises our education system? Who decides what is to be taught? Who has a material interest in not letting certain things be known about? The employers, the landowners and the bourgeoisie. For as long as we continue to allow them, it's obvious that they'll carry on doing what they consider to be correct. Can you imagine what would happen if they all suddenly went crazy and began telling the history of how, in the 14th century, in Lombardy and in Piedmont, there was a full-blooded revolution, during which, in the name of Jesus Christ, people began to set up communes in which all people were equal, everybody loved each other, and nobody exploited anyone else? What would happen? The children would get all excited, and start shouting: 'Long live Fra' Dolcino! Down with the Pope!' And, my goodness, this sort of thing cannot be allowed…!

Of course, I'm overstating the case, from my natural love of polemic. The truth is that in some of our better schools, this information can just about be found in the history books. Admittedly, only in footnotes. Footnotes which go something like this: 'Fra' Dolcino, a heretic, was burned alive in 1306, together with his woman friend.' You see? The children learn that Fra' Dolcino was a heretic. Probably because he had a woman friend!

Now I would like to perform the Boniface VIII sketch. It begins with an extremely ancient liturgical chant in Catalan, from the Pyrenees. During this chanting, the Pope dresses himself for a very important ceremony. You should bear in mind that Boniface VIII had a habit: that of nailing certain monks to the doors of the houses of the nobility in certain cities… by their tongues. You see, these 'Poor Brothers', who were linked with the Cathars and other heretical movements, had an unfortunate habit of going round speaking ill of the nobility. So the Pope grabbed them, and… whap…! (*He mimes the action of nailing somebody up by their tongue*) Not the Pope personally, of course, because he got upset at the sight of blood: he had men employed to do it… He wasn't one to keep such pleasures all to himself…

Another story is told about Boniface, which will give you an idea of the sort of man he was. He organised an orgy on Good Friday, 1301. Among the many processions taking place in Rome that day, there was one organised by the Cathars, who used their liturgical chanting in order to get a few underhand digs at the Pope. They said:

> 'Jesus Christ was a poor person. He went around without even a cloak. But there is a person who does have a cloak, and that cloak is full of precious stones. There is someone who sits on a throne made all of gold, while Christ walked with bare feet. Christ, who was God, the Eternal Father, came to earth to be a man; there is somebody who is not even a man, and who fancies himself so much as the Eternal Father that he has himself carried around on a litter.'

I ask you! Boniface, of course, who was pretty sharp, thought to himself: 'You see, they're picking on me! So? I'll show them what I think of them!' So he organised an orgy. On the very day of Good Friday. He summoned a number of prostitutes, a number of women from good families (which often meant the same thing), bishops and cardinals, and it appears that they all set about indulging themselves in some pretty low-life goings-on. To such an extent that all the courts of Europe were scandalised, including that of Henry III of England, who, according to chroniclers of the time, was a fairly gross king as kings go. In fact, they say that he used to amuse his barons during banquets by blowing out a candle with a burp at three metres distance! In fact, one of the chroniclers claimed – not that I personally believe him – that he was able to blow out candles with a kind of ricochet effect... He would aim his burp against a wall, and it would bounce off... (*He mimes*) Crash, bang, wallop! This of course is the English sense of humour, the subtleties of which we are not in a position to grasp. We just have to accept it for what it is, a bit like cricket.

BONIFACE VIII

He plays the part of Boniface VIII. He mimes the gestures of praying and chanting.

> On the Day of Judgement,
> An eternal King will come,
> He who has created everything,
> Fleshed in our mortal flesh,

> Verily he will come,
> From heaven, on the day…

He breaks off, turns to an imaginary CLERIC *and takes his mitre. He begins chanting again.*

> Thus the judgement will not be…
> A mighty sign will be given…

He mimes taking the mitre off his head.

Oh, this is really heavy! No, let's go… I must carry on…

He mimes taking another item of headgear.

Ah, this one will do.

He puts it on his head, and begins chanting again.

> On the Day of Judgement…

He breaks off.

The mirror…

He mimes looking at himself in the mirror.

It's crooked, you see! …The gloves!

He starts walking again, trying to get one of his gloves on. He chants.

> Thus the judgement will not be…
> A mighty sign will be given…

Where's the other one… ? Why only one glove? I've got two hands, you know! I haven't only got one hand… ! Am I supposed to cut the other one off?

He chants.

> The sun will fade in splendour,
> The earth will tremble with fear…

He gives an order.

The cloak, the big cloak…

He mimes taking a large, heavy cloak.

> On the Day of Judgement
> He will appear, who…

Oof, this is really heavy…!

He tries getting it around his shoulders. He beckons his ACOLYTES *to help him.*

He will appear, who created all things.

Push, all together, let's go…

His chant slows.

Come on! Are you going to get a move on? Why aren't you singing too?! Do I have to do everything myself? Sing, wear the cloak, wear the hat… Let's go! Now, stop a minute. Let's start again!

Still turning to the imaginary CLERICS.

And you, sing! Let's have…you, first voice…

He chants as if he is trying to get a particular CLERIC *to chant.*

　　…created a-a-a-all things.

He continues, nodding his head in time.

　　An eternal King will come…

Second voice!

He points to another CLERIC.

　　Fleshed in our mortal flesh…

Third voice!

He turns to the first CLERIC.

　　He will come for sure, from heaven…

He breaks off, fed up.

Out of tune!! Come on, let's all sing together.

He chants, his voice going into the high register. Then he stops abruptly.

　　To bring the Day of Judgement…

Who trod on my cloak?!

He spins round, furious.

Was it you? You there – squeaker! Miserable wretch… He won't chant and he won't push… Right, let's go. Let's have the Alleluiah.

He breaks off, incredulous.

Don't you even know what the Alleluiah is? …The Alleluiah is the twiddly bit that goes up and down in the middle. Right, let's go…

　　On the Day of Judgement
　　He will appear who has created everything

He trills his words and drags his cloak. He stops, exhausted.

Oh, what a lousy job, being Pope!

He gives a final heave, to get his cloak on.

> An eternal King will come,
> Fleshed in our mortal flesh...

Again he turns to a CLERIC.

The ring!

Still chanting, he slips the ring on. He admires it, and breathes on it as he warbles and trills.

Look how it sparkles!

He gives an order.

And the other ring. The big one... for my thumb...

He puts the ring on his thumb, and continues chanting.

...Will come for sure, from heaven

The crozier, my staff!

Shouting.

No, the staff... Not the one for beating people with. Get on with it. I want the one with the curly bit on top!

He indicates the curly top of the crozier. He starts chanting again.

> Will come for sure, from heaven...

Are we ready? Can we start? Eh? Let's go. Together. Don't push like that, wretch; do you want to send me sprawling in the mud? And you, deaf-ears, squeaker, watch out! Right. Let's mark time: two steps marking time before we go: One, two, *now*, the Alleluiah!

He chants.

> The babies who have not been born
> Will cry out from inside their mothers.
> Everyone will weep and cry.
> Help us, oh all-powerful God.

I'm in good voice today!

Hey! Where are you all going? Where are you off to? Where's everyone gone?! You can't just leave me here like this! I am the Pope! I am Boniface! I'm not just some old horse and cart driver...

Who is that? Who...? Who's that with the cross? Jesus? Ah, Christ! Jesus Christ... Look, look what a terrible state he's in! Now I see why they call him 'poor Christ'... Good heavens... Look at the state of him...

Damn! Let's get moving! I don't like looking at things like this.

He pretends to reply to a CLERIC *who has a different opinion.*

You say it would be better if I went over to him...? So that I can show people that I'm a good person, so that I can show myself helping to carry his cross... Well now, that would be a good idea. Everyone will applaud me, saying: 'What a good fellow that Boniface is' ...Alright, then, let's make them happy, these simpletons... Let's go.

He mimes taking his things off.

There you go, take the cloak... Take it... And the staff... I'd better go now. You won't believe this, but my legs are shaking... Hello Jesus, how are you? Jesus... Don't you recognise me? I am Boniface... Boniface... the Pope... What do you mean, who's the Pope?! You know, he's the shepherd, the one who follows on from St Peter, with all the others, at the end of the line... Don't you recognise me? Ah, it must be because of this big hat... Weeell, that was because it was raining... Anyway...

Turning to the CLERIC.

Come and take all this stuff off... And the ring! Don't let him see that I've got rings...

He mimes taking off all his frippery.

Don't let him see all this glittery stuff... He's got terrible fixed ideas, that one! A very odd character... Come on, take my shoes off... quick! He likes to see people with bare feet... Come on, quick! Give me something so that I can dirty myself... Some earth for my face.

He smears his face with mud.

Come on, dirty me all over. He likes people like this. What do you expect – he's crazy!

He turns to CHRIST.

Do you recognise me now? I am your son... Humble as I am, I come before you. Jesus... Look, I kneel before you... I, who have never kneeled before anyone; I, before whom... Jesus... Jesus... For God's sake, pay attention for a moment! What is this – he's ignoring me!! Let's have some manners, for heaven's sake! As I was saying...

He stops, as if CHRIST *had interrupted him.*

Me... Me? What did you say? That I have killed monks? Me? That I have done wrong? It's not true! This is gossip. These are lies put round by malcontents, out of jealousy...

Pointing at him angrily.

I've heard a few things about you too, my friend, but I don't believe them! My goodness, those are bad people, you know...

He kneels down, in desperation.

Jesus, Jesus, look into my eyes. I love you and I have always had nothing but good feelings for the monks...

He turns to the imaginary CLERIC.

Go and get me a monk, quickly!

To CHRIST.

I love them...

To the CLERIC.

Where are you supposed to go and find monks? Go to the prison! It's full of them!

To CHRIST.

Jesus, I... Jesus, look, a monk, look, how splendid...

He mimes embracing the MONK *and kissing him, and turns his face away in disgust.*

What a stink!

To CHRIST.

Jesus, let me help you carry your cross, because I am strong, and you're getting tired... I am used to it... I'm an ox, you know... I wear really heavy cloaks! Let me... Out of the way, Cyrenian!

He mimes chasing off the CYRENIAN *and taking his place carrying the cross.*

I'll help you… No, it's no trouble… No, don't push! Jesus, good…

He's sent flying headlong by a great kick.

Christ! Kicking me?! Me, Boniface! The Prince! Ah, right! Rabble…! Ne'er-do-well…! I tell you, if your father gets to hear of this… Wretch! Donkey of all donkeys! Listen, I don't mind telling you that it will give me great pleasure to see you nailed up; and this very day I am going to get myself drunk! I am going dancing… dancing! And I am going with whores!!! Because I, I am Boniface… I am a prince! Cloak, mitre, staff, rings… and everything! Look how they glisten… Rabble! I, I am Boniface! Sing!

He exits, triumphant, and strutting, chanting at the top of his voice.

> On the Day of Judgement will appear
> He who has created everything.
> An eternal King will come,
> Fleshed in our mortal flesh,
> He will come from heaven for sure…

THE PASSION PLAYS

DEATH AND THE FOOL

In an inn, a number of layabouts are playing cards with the Fool.

FOOL: The Horse on the Ass, and the Virgin on the Lecher means that I take the lot. Ha, ha! You thought you were going to pluck me like a chicken, didn't you?! So what do you think of that, then?

He deals the cards.

FIRST PLAYER: The game's not over yet... Wait a while, before you start to crow.

FOOL: Not at all, I shall sing as I like... and dance. Oh, what lovely cards. Good evening, your majesty, Mr King, would you mind going and taking the crown off that ugly bastard friend of mine?

He slaps a card down on the table.

SECOND PLAYER: Ha, ha! You've come unstuck with your King, because now I cap him with an Emperor!

FOOL: Oh, oh, look what the Emperor has done! Alright, I'll cap you with this. (*He turns his back and puts his backside on the table*) And then, for good measure, I'll put down this Murderer, who will slaughter your Emperor like a pig.

FIRST PLAYER: And I've got a Captain, to arrest your Murderer...

FOOL: And I shall bring in War, so that your Captain has to go away.

SECOND PLAYER: And I'll lay Famine, Cholera and

Pestilence, which will end the War.

FOOL: Well, then you'd better take your umbrella, because I'm going to bring a storm… this storm… Psssss… Rain and flood!

He takes a mouthful from his glass, and sprays it over everyone in sight.

FIRST PLAYER: Oh, Matazone, you wretch, what are you, crazy?

FOOL: Of course I'm crazy, ha, ha… If *matto* means crazy, and you call me Matazone, then I must be crazy… And I win the card-game with my Flood, which washes away all pestilences.

LANDLADY: Do you mind stopping all this row, because there's people in the big room next door who're just going to sit down to eat.

FOOL: Who are they?

LANDLADY: I don't know… I've never seen these fellows in my inn before, in Emmaeus. They call them the Apostles…

SECOND PLAYER: Ah! Those are the twelve fellows who follow the one from Nazareth.

FOOL: Yes, Jesus. He must be the one in the middle there… Look, what a pleasant fellow! Hello, Jesus of Nazareth… Hello, there. Enjoy your dinner! Did you see that? He winked at me… What a lovely fellow!

THIRD PLAYER: Twelve and one makes thirteen… Oh, thirteen of them sitting down to eat… That's bound to bring bad luck!

FOOL: Well, seeing that they're mad…! Wait a minute, and I shall say a spell to keep away the evil eye. (*He sings*) Thirteen at table to eat does not bring bad luck; evil eye, stay away, as I touch this bum!

He pinches the LANDLADY's *backside.*

LANDLADY: Behave yourself, Matazone, because you'll make me spill all this hot water.

FIRST PLAYER: Hot water? What are they going to do with that?

LANDLADY: I think they're going to wash their feet.

SECOND PLAYER: Wash their feet before eating? Hey, they really are crazy! Matazone, you should go and join them, because they're the right sort of company for the likes of you.

FOOL: You've said it, you're right. I'll win this game, and with the money that I win off you, I'll go into the big room, and drink it all away with them. And you won't be able to come – you can't join the madmen, because you're all sons of bitches and crooks.

They shuffle the cards.

THIRD PLAYER: Come on, let's start. Play your hand, because I'm really looking forward to seeing how you think you're going to win.

FOOL: While we're on the subject of crooks, what ever happened to the Fool that I had among my cards?

SECOND PLAYER: Someone give him a mirror, so that he can look at himself. Then you'll find the face of your Fool.

FIRST PLAYER: Don't waste time, let's get on playing… (*He plays a card*) A Knight with his sword.

SECOND PLAYER: A Queen with her sceptre.

FOOL: The Witch with her goat…

THIRD PLAYER: The Innocent Child.

FIRST PLAYER: God Almighty.

FOOL: Justice and Reason.

SECOND PLAYER: The Trickster and the Lawyer.

THIRD PLAYER: The Executioner and the Hanged Man.

FOOL: The Pope and the Popess.

FIRST PLAYER: The Priest giving Mass.

SECOND PLAYER: A Good and Happy Life.

THIRD PLAYER: Death in black and white.

SECOND PLAYER: All my cards are gone. My dear Fool, you have lost.

FOOL: How can that be! How could I lose?

FIRST PLAYER: How could you lose? Because, my dear, idiotic Fool, you don't know how to play. Let's have you now. Out with your money!

FOOL: You hunchbacked horror! You've stripped me completely, and just think, I was sure that I had that card here, the card of Death. I know I had it here somewhere.

At the back of the stage, DEATH *appears: a fair-skinned woman, with her eyes circled in black.*

SECOND PLAYER: Oh, Mother, who is that?!

The FOOL *has his back to* DEATH. *He is intent on counting out his money.*

THIRD PLAYER: The Witch…! Death!

Everybody except the FOOL *exits, running.*

FOOL: Yes, Death! There you are… I *did* have it! Goodness, it's turning cold… Where have you all disappeared off to? This cold is enough to chill you to the bone. Shut that door! (*He barely notices* DEATH) Good day. All the windows are shut… Where on earth can this freezing cold be coming from? (*He sees* DEATH *standing there*) Good day, good evening, good night, madam. Excuse me. (*He gets up to leave*) Since my friends have all decided to leave… (*He has forgotten his money on the table*) Were you looking for somebody? The landlady is there in the big room, serving the Apostles, and taking them a basin to wash their feet in. If you want to join them, feel free, don't stand on ceremony. Oh, my teeth are chattering!

DEATH: No, thank you. I prefer to wait here.

FOOL: Alright. Would you like to sit down? Take this chair. It's still warm, I warmed it up myself! Excuse my asking, madam, but now that I see you from close up, I have a feeling that we've met somewhere before.

DEATH: That is impossible, for people who meet me meet me only once.

FOOL: Ah yes? Only once? And you have a slightly foreign way of speaking. It sounds a bit Tuscan. Or Ferrarese? Or Roman? Or from Sicily? Or maybe Cremona? Because the Cremonese are more foreign than anyone, even more foreign than the people of Lodi, who are foreigners even in their own town! Anyway, madam, I hope you won't mind my saying so, but you look a bit down in the dumps, a little pale in the face, compared with the last time we met.

DEATH: Are you saying that I look pale?

FOOL: Yes. I hope I haven't offended you?

DEATH: No, I have been pale for all time. Pallor is my natural colour.

FOOL: Naturally pale, eh? Ah, that's who you look like! You're the spitting image of that picture on the playing card!

DEATH: True. I am Death.

FOOL: Death? Ah, so you're Death? Oh, what a combination! Death! Well, pleased to meet you... I am Matazone, the Fool.

DEATH: Aren't you afraid?

FOOL: Me, scared? No. I am a Fool, and everyone knows that, just like in the Tarot cards, the Fool has nothing to fear from Death. On the contrary, he goes looking for her, to marry her, because, joined together, they can beat any other card, even the card of Love!

DEATH: If you're not afraid, then how come your leg is all trembling?

FOOL: My leg? Ah, that's because this isn't my own leg. I lost my own leg on the battlefield... and so I took another one from a Captain, who had been killed, and his leg was still alive and moving, like the tail of a freshly killed lizard.

Anyway, I cut his leg off, and I stuck it on in place of my own, stuck it on with spit. There you are, look, you can see that it's not mine… It's longer than the other one by about a span, and it makes me limp. Hey! Behave yourself, Captain's leg! Because you shouldn't be afraid of such an illustrious and noble madonna… Let's have you!

DEATH: That is very kind of you, to call me an illustrious madonna.

FOOL: Oh, believe me, I'm not just standing on ceremony. As far as I'm concerned, I swear it, you really are illustrious, and very nice too. And I'm very glad that you came here looking for me, because I like you. So much so that I would like to buy you a drink, if you'll permit me.

DEATH: Willingly! Did you say that you liked me?

FOOL: Certainly! I like everything about you, your scent of chrysanthemums, and the paleness of your face, because, where I come from, we have a saying: 'A woman with a skin the colour of whitewash is a woman who will never tire of making love.'

DEATH: Oh, you're making me all bashful, Fool – for so you are! Nobody has ever made me blush like this before.

FOOL: Go ahead and blush, because you are a pure and virgin lady. It is true that you have embraced many men, but you only embrace them once… And none of those was worthy of coming to lie next to you, because none of them values you or bears you a sincere and honest love.

DEATH: It is true, nobody values me!

FOOL: That is because you are too modest, and you don't blow your own trumpet or bang your drum to announce your arrival, for all that you are Queen, Queen of the World! I drink to your health, Queen!

DEATH: The health of Death? I can't make out whether you're just mad, or a poet!

FOOL: Both. Because every poet is a fool, and every fool a poet. Drink, my pale lady, because this wine will give you a bit of colour.

DEATH: Oh, how good the wine is!

FOOL: And how could it not be good? It is the same wine that the Nazarene is drinking in the big room next door, and he's a man who really knows about wine! He's a big connoisseur, that one!

DEATH: Which one of them is the fellow from Nazareth?

FOOL: The young one sitting in the middle, the one with the big shiny eyes.

DEATH: Oh, he's a fine looking fellow, and so sweet.

FOOL: Yes, he's a fine man, but I hope you're not trying to make me jealous. You're not going to do me the discourtesy of leaving me, to go with them? Because then I would burst into tears.

DEATH: So, you rogue, you're trying to flatter me, eh?

She removes her black veil.

FOOL: Me? Flatter? Flatter a lady whom not even popes or emperors can conquer? (DEATH *reveals herself; she has blond hair*) Oh, how beautiful you are, with that golden hair. I would happily gather all the flowers on earth and cover you with them, all over, a great heap, and then I would dive in and find you under that heap, and I would strip you of those flowers... and of everything else too!

DEATH: My dear Fool, these words are making me all hot and flustered, and I must say, I'm sorry, because I would have been glad to remain in your company, and then to take you away with me.

FOOL: Wasn't that the reason you came? To take me away with you? Ah! So you didn't come for me... Ha, ha! And to think that I thought... Ah, how ridiculous. Oh well, I've really enjoyed our conversation. I'm really happy... Ha, ha!

DEATH: Now I see that you are a liar, and that you were only pretending to love me, so that you could get on the right side of me, out of your fear of me... of Death...

FOOL: No, my pale Lady, you don't understand. I am happy because you didn't come to me for any particular reason, because you didn't just stay in my company because you had a job to do, drawing out my final breath. You stayed with me because you like me, isn't that so? You find me a pleasant fellow, don't you, pale lady? But, what's happening? What are those tears welling up in your eyes? Oh, come on, that's too much. Death, crying! Have I offended you?

DEATH: No, not offended me. You have only softened my heart. I am crying because I am sorry for that boy Jesus, who is so sweet, because he is the one that I am supposed to take away to die.

FOOL: Ah, so you came for him? For Christ? Well, I'm sorry too. Poor lad, with that well-meaning face of his. And what illness is going to carry him off? A stomach illness? A heart disease? A disease of the lungs?

DEATH: Cross sickness...

FOOL: Cross sickness...? You mean that he's going to be nailed up? Oh, poor Christ, why couldn't you be called something else! Listen, pale Lady, do me a favour. Let me go and warn him, so that he can prepare himself for this terrible suffering.

DEATH: It is pointless you warning him, because he knows already. He has known it since the day he was born, that one day he would be stretched on the cross.

FOOL: He knows it, and still he stays there, chatting, and smiling happily with his friends? Oh, he must be even more crazy than me!

DEATH: It is true, what you say... And how could he not be crazy, he who so loves mankind, even those who are going to take him to the cross, even Judas who will betray him!

FOOL: Ah, so it will be Judas? That fellow with the Judas face over there, the one at the corner of the table. I might have known it! Wait while I go and give the wretch a smack round the ear and spit in his eye.

DEATH: Leave him be. It's not worth it, because you would have to spit in all their eyes, because when the time comes, they will all turn their backs on him.

FOOL: All of them? Even Saint Peter?

DEATH: He will be the first, and will betray him thrice thereafter. Come on, let's not sit here thinking about it. Pour me a glass of wine, because I want to get drunk, and escape from this sadness.

FOOL: Better to have a happy Death! So: let's drink and chase off the gloom. Fine pale lady, come and let's be merry. Take off your cloak, so that I can see your arms, the colour of the moon... Oh, how beautiful they are... And undo your jacket in front, because I want to feast my eyes on those two silver apples, that look like the stars of Diana.

DEATH: No, please, Fool, I am still a maid and a virgin, and you're putting me to shame, because no man has ever touched me naked!

FOOL: But I am not a man, I am a Fool, and Death would not be committing a sin to make love with a Fool, with a crazy lunatic such as me. Don't be afraid, because I shall turn out all the lights, and leave only one burning, and we shall go and dance some pretty steps that I shall teach you, and I shall make you sing with sighs and amorous swoonings.

MARY HEARS OF THE SENTENCE
IMPOSED ON HER SON

Mary is with Joanna, and meets Amelia in the street.

AMELIA: Good day, Mary… Good day, Joanna.

MARY: Good day, Amelia, are you going shopping?

AMELIA: No, I already did my shopping this morning… I've got something I have to tell you, Joanna.

JOANNA: Tell me. Excuse me a moment, Mary.

They move to one side, and talk excitedly

MARY: Where are all these people going? What's happening down there?

JOANNA: It must be somebody's wedding…

AMELIA: Yes… It's a wedding… That's just where I'm coming from now.

MARY: Oh, Joanna, let's go and look, because I love weddings. Is the bride young? And who is the bridegroom?

JOANNA: I don't know… I think it must be somebody from out of town.

AMELIA: Let's go, Mary. Let's not waste time with weddings, let's go home, because we still have to put the water on the stove for the stew.

MARY: Wait, listen. They're cursing!

JOANNA: Oh, they must be swearing because they're happy…

MARY: No, it sounds as if they're really angry. They're shouting: 'Sorcerer!' Yes, there it is again. I can hear it clearly. Listen. Who are they taking it out on?

JOANNA: Oh, now I think about it, it isn't a wedding at all; they are taking it out on somebody they discovered last night, dancing with a goat, which turned out to be the Devil.

MARY: Ah, so that's why they're calling him 'Sorcerer'.

JOANNA: Yes, that must be it... But let's not delay, Mary. Let's go home, because you shouldn't look at things like that, because you might get the evil eye on you.

MARY: There's a cross sticking out over the people's heads! And look, another two crosses!

JOANNA: Yes, those other two are for two thieves...

MARY: Poor people... Are they going to crucify all three...? Just think of their poor mothers! And to think that she, poor woman, probably doesn't even know that they are killing her son.

Enter MARY MAGDALENE, *running*.

MARY MAGDALENE: Oh Mary! Your son Jesus...

JOANNA: Yes, yes, she knows it already. (*Aside*) Shut up, you fool.

MARY: What do I know already? What's happened to my son?

JOANNA: Nothing... What should have happened to him, you blessed woman? It's only that... Ah, didn't I tell you? Oh, how forgetful of me... It completely went out of my head, to tell you that he, your son, told me that he wouldn't be home to eat at noon, because he had to go into the mountains to tell parables.

MARY: Is that what you too came to tell me?

MARY MAGDALENE: Yes, that's it, Madonna.

MARY: Thank the Lord... You arrived in such a hurry, dear girl, that I took a terrible fright... I began to imagine all kinds of terrible things... How silly we mothers are sometimes... we get all worried over nothing!

JOANNA: Yes, how stupid of her, coming running like crazy, just to tell you something so trivial.

MARY: Alright, Joanna... Don't start shouting at her now... After all, she was good enough to come and give me the message. I thank you, young lady... What's your name? I seem to know you...

MARY MAGDALENE: I am Magdalene...

MARY: Magdalene? Which Magdalene? The one who...

JOANNA: Yes, she's the one... The prostitute. Let's leave, let's go home, because it's best that we're not seen with people like her. It gives a bad impression.

MARY MAGDALENE: But I don't work any more.

JOANNA: That must be because you can't find any dirty men to get your hands on... Leave us, hussy!

MARY: No, don't chase her off, poor girl... If my beloved Jesus has faith enough in her as to send her to give me a message, it's a sign that she's seen the error of her ways, isn't it, Magdalene...?

MARY MAGDALENE: Yes, I'm more sensible now.

JOANNA: You really believe that? The truth is that your son is too good. He lets himself be overcome by pity, and everyone takes advantage of him! He's always surrounded by a crowd of ne'er-do-wells, people without work or skills, starvelings, wretches and whores... like this one!

MARY: Joanna, those are wicked words! My son always says that it is for them, above all others, for them, the wretched and the lost, that he came into this world, in order to give them hope.

JOANNA: Alright, agreed. But don't you understand that it creates a bad impression. People start talking behind your back... Just think, with all the proper people that there are in this town, the gentlemen and the ladies, the doctors, the nobles... And he, with his gentle, wise and learned ways, could command immediate respect, and would be honoured, and could get help if he needed. But no, my goodness; he goes and takes up with lousy rogues!

MARY: Listen how they are shouting, and laughing... But I can't see the cross.

JOANNA: Leaving aside the fact that it would also be better if he stopped always talking ill of bishops and priests... because they don't forgive such things lightly!

MARY: There they are again, the three crosses...

JOANNA: One day they're going to make him pay for all that... They'll find some way of doing him harm!

MARY: Do harm to my son? Why? Because he is so good. Doesn't he help everyone, even those who don't ask? And everybody likes him! Listen, they've started sneering and jeering again... One of them must have fallen down. Everyone likes my son, don't they...

MARY MAGDALENE: Yes, I like him too, a lot!

JOANNA: Oh yes, everybody knows the way that you like him, the way that *you* like Mary's son!

MARY MAGDALENE: I have more love for him than I would have even for a brother! And now...

JOANNA: Now... ! What about before, then!?

MARY: Joanna, stop tormenting the poor girl... What's she ever done to you...? Can't you see that she's upset? Why are they shouting so much? And so what if this young girl had the kind of love for him that normal women have for men that they like...? Well? Isn't my son a man too, as well as being God? He has the eyes, the hands, the feet of a man... He is a man all over, even down to his pain and happinesses! So, it'll be up to my son to decide... And he will know the right thing to do, when the time comes, if he decides to get married. As far as I am concerned, anybody whom he chooses, I shall cherish as if she were my own daughter. And I hope that this day comes soon... Because he's already thirty-three, and it's time that he started raising a family... Oh, what a horrible noise they're making with all that shouting down there, and how black that cross is! I would so much like to have his children running around the house... to play with, and cradle... I know a lot of lullabies... I would really spoil them, and tell them stories, the kind of stories that always have a happy ending!

JOANNA: Yes, but that's enough standing here and dreaming, Mary... Come along, because at this rate we won't even be in time to prepare the evening meal.

MARY: I'm not hungry... I don't know why... I've a bit of stomach cramp... I'm going to have to go down there, to see what's going on.

JOANNA: No, don't go... That sort of scene just makes people sad. You'll feel heartbroken all day. Your son won't like it. At this very moment, he could be at home waiting for us, starving hungry.

MARY: But he sent a message to say that he wouldn't be home!

JOANNA: He might have changed his mind. You know what children are like. You wait at home for them, and they don't come... And then they always turn up when you least expect them! And you have to be there, all ready, with the food on the stove.

MARY: Yes... you're right. Would you like to come as well, Magdalene, and share a bowl of soup?

MARY MAGDALENE: I'd love to, if it's no trouble.

VERONICA *crosses the stage*.

MARY: What has happened to that woman, with that bloodied towel that she's carrying...? Good woman, have you hurt yourself?

VERONICA: No, not me... It was one of those that they've got down at the crosses, the one they're calling 'Sorcerer'... He's not a sorcerer, though. He's a holy man, a saint, for sure, because you can see it from his sweet eyes... I cleaned his bloody face for him...

MARY: Oh, you kind woman...

VERONICA: …with this towel, and a miracle happened… He left the imprint of his face on the towel. It could almost be a portrait.

MARY: Let me see.

JOANNA: Don't, Mary. Curiosity is not good for you.

MARY: I'm not curious… I just feel that I must see it…

VERONICA: Alright, I'll let you see it. But first, you must cross yourself… There, he's the Son of God!

MARY: Oh, my son! Oh, it's my son!

She runs off, in desperation.

JOANNA: Now look what you've done… Wretched woman!

VERONICA: But I didn't realise she was his mother!

THE FOOL BENEATH THE CROSS,
LAYING A WAGER

Onstage, the FOOL, SOLDIERS *and four* CRUCIFIERS.
They hang up a sheet, behind which JESUS *is made to undress.*

FOOL: Come on, Ladies! You ladies who love this Christ,
come and feast your eyes on him... Come and see your
dear one all naked as he undressed... Two pence for a
look... Come on, Ladies! He looks almost good enough to
eat! They say that he was the Son of God. To me he looks
the same as any other man, just the same! Two pence for a
look at him, Ladies! Doesn't anyone want to take up my
offer – only two pence? Well, it's a holiday today, so I'll cut
my prices... Come along you, I'll let you look for free...
Oh, what a miserable face... Come here. It's a chance not
to be missed... Aren't you that Mary Magdalene who was
so much in love with him that, when you couldn't find a
towel to dry his feet, you dried them with your hair? Well,
so much the worse for you; because now the law says that
here in this place of sin we are to dress him, dress him in a
little apron that'll make him look like a ballerina!

Is the chief player ready? Pull up the cloth so that we can
start the show! Scene One: the Son of God, a gentleman
knight... See his crown! He's going a-jousting. He'll be
riding a fine horse made out of wood... And so that he does
not fall off, we are going to nail him to the saddle... by his
hands and feet!

CHIEF CRUCIFIER: Stop clowning around and come here
to give us a hand... Put a rope round his wrists, one on
either side, so that we can stretch him out properly... But
leave his palms free, so that we can get the nails in. I'll

hammer the right one in, and…

FIRST CRUCIFIER: And I'll do the other. Throw me a nail… I already have a hammer.

SECOND CRUCIFIER: Oh, what an ugly great nail! Let's have a bet. I bet that I can hammer it right home with seven blows.

FIRST CRUCIFIER: And I shall do it in six. We bet?

SECOND CRUCIFIER: Agreed. Right, you two, move aside, so that we can put the wings on this Angel, so that he can fly up into the sky, like Icarus.

THIRD CRUCIFIER: All heave together… Together, I said! You're tipping him off. Gently, so that he stays in the saddle, this knight of ours… Over to me a little… Right! I'm right on the mark now.

SECOND CRUCIFIER: I'm not, though. You've made the holes too far apart… Hey, you, pull! Go on! What's the matter, did you eat cheese for lunch? A bit of effort!

FIRST CRUCIFIER: You say 'a bit of effort', but we'll end up by tearing the ligaments in his shoulders and elbows.

THIRD CRUCIFIER: Don't worry… They're not your ligaments! Pull! A bit of effort!

JESUS *groans with pain; the* WOMEN *groan in chorus, and in counterpoint*

FIRST CRUCIFIER: Oh, did you hear that crack?

SECOND CRUCIFIER: Yes… horrible, wasn't it! It sends shivers down your spine. But at least he's stretched out to the right length. Now I'm over the hole too.

FIRST CRUCIFIER: Right. Keep the tension on the rope. You, raise the hammer, and we'll start off together.

SECOND CRUCIFIER: Mind you don't bang your thumbs!

The others laugh.

THIRD CRUCIFIER: Open your paw. I promise I won't tickle you… Oh, just look at that hand! Look at his

life-line. It's so long that you'd think that this light was
going to live for at least another 50 years... That's what you
get for believing in old wives' tales, you!

SECOND CRUCIFIER: Shut your mouth and raise your
hammer.

FIRST CRUCIFIER: I'm ready.

THIRD CRUCIFIER: Right, let's go. Give the first blow... (*A
thud*) Ohioa ahh! To make a hole in his palms!

CHIEF CRUCIFIER: (*In counterpoint with* CHRIST's
screams) Oooh! He's trembling all over. Calm down. Now the
second blow: Ohaioaohh! To spread the bones a bit.

> Ohoh And now he's spitting blood.
> Give the third blow.
> Ohahiohoh
> This nail will deflower you.
> Ohoh you who have never had a woman.
> The fourth is a present from the soldiers
> Ohahiohoh
> Whom you told not to kill
> Ohahiohoh!
> And to love their enemies like brothers.
> Ohahiohoh
> The fifth is from the bishops in the synagogue
> Ohahiohoh!
> Who you said were false and damned.
> Ohahiohoh!
> The sixth is a present from the rich
> Ohahiohoh!
> Who you said could not go to heaven
> Ohahiohoh!
> When you told them about the camel.
> Ohahiohoh!
> The seventh blow is from the impostors
> Ohahiohoh!
> Whom you told that it didn't matter if they prayed
> Ohahiohoh!
> Because the Lord would ignore them.

FIRST CRUCIFIER: I've won! You owe me a drink. Don't forget it.

SECOND CRUCIFIER: Let's drink to the health of this gentleman and his misfortunes! How are you, your majesty? Do you have your steed well in hand? Right, let's off to the jousting, but without shield or lance this time!

CHIEF CRUCIFIER: Have you released the rope from his wrists? Well done, my barons... Now, tighten this belt around his chest, because we don't want him falling on us as we hoist him up, this champion of ours! Then, once we've got his feet nailed down, we'll remove it.

SECOND CRUCIFIER: Come here all of you... Spit on your hands, because now we've got to hoist up our greasy pole! Come over here with that rope, and hook it over the crossbeam... And you too, Matazone. Climb up on top of the ladder so that you can be ready to hold it.

FOOL: I'm sorry, I can't help you: that fellow has never done anything to harm me.

SECOND CRUCIFIER: Oh rubbish... He hasn't done anything to us either: we're just crucifying him to pass the time, ha, ha! And they're giving us ten pence a head for the trouble... Come on, give us your hand, and then afterwards we'll do you the honour of playing a game of dice with you.

FOOL: Ah well, if it's for a game of dice, then that's a different matter. Look, I'm on the ladder already... You can begin!

FIRST CRUCIFIER: Bravo! Everyone ready to begin? Right, let's go... Please, all pull together, one long pull at a time. I'll give you the rhythm.

> Ho, let's pull – Ehiee
> Up this ship's mast – ohoho
> On it, as a banner – ohoh
> We've stuck a fool – ohoho
>
> Ho let's pull – Ehiee

> Up this big greasy pole – ohoho
> With Christ in the crow's nest – ohoho
>
> Ho, what a pole – Ahaaa
> It pierces the sky – ohoho
> It rains blood – ohoho
> Our father weeps – ohoho
>
> Be merry, be merry – Ohee
> For we have found that brave lad – ohoho
> Who made himself a slave – ohoho
> In order to clothe us anew – ohoho

Stop. That'll do. I think that's good and firm. Right, now get the dice out so that we can play.

They play at dice, and at Tarot, and the FOOL *wins Christ's tunic, and the* CRUCIFIERS *pay.*

FOOL: If you want all your money back, I'll let you have it willingly, including the necklace, and the ring. Look. And I'll throw this in too.

FIRST CRUCIFIER: And what do you want in exchange for all this stuff?

FOOL: That man...

SECOND CRUCIFIER: Christ?

FOOL: Yes. I want you to let me take him down from the cross.

CHIEF CRUCIFIER: Alright, wait till he's dead, and he's all yours...

FOOL: No. I want him now, while he's still alive.

FIRST CRUCIFIER: Oh, you must be the fool of all fools! Do you want all us four to end up, up there, in his place?

FOOL: No, you needn't worry that anything's going to happen to you. All we have to do is put someone else up there, of about the same build, and nobody will notice the change... because anyway people look much the same when they're crucified.

FIRST CRUCIFIER: That's true enough… Stripped like that he looks like a fish on a griddle…

CHIEF CRUCIFIER: That's as may be. But I don't agree. Anyway, who did you have in mind to put in his place?

FOOL: Judas!

CHIEF CRUCIFIER: Judas? You mean the one who…

FOOL: Yes, that treacherous apostle who hanged himself in despair from the figtree behind the hedge fifty yards down the road.

CHIEF CRUCIFIER: Hey, get a move on, hurry up, let's go and strip him, because he must still have those thirty pieces of silver in his pocket.

FOOL: I wouldn't bother, if I were you… Because he threw them away into a thicket right away.

CHIEF CRUCIFIER: How do you know?

FOOL: I know because I went and picked up that money, piece by piece. Look how my arms got scratched in the process!

CHIEF CRUCIFIER: I'm not interested in your scratches. Let's see the money. Oh! And it's all silver! Look how splendid! How heavy! And what a chinking sound…

FOOL: Alright. You can keep them. These are yours too, if you'll do that swap. I'm ready.

CHIEF CRUCIFIER: So are we.

FOOL: Right, so go and get that hanged Judas at once, while I work out how to get Christ down.

FIRST CRUCIFIER: And what if the Centurion arrives and finds you in the middle of taking Christ off the cross?

FOOL: You tell him that it was my idea, and that I'm a Fool. And that you're not guilty. But don't stand there wasting time. Go!

CHIEF CRUCIFIER: Yes, yes, we're going. And let's hope that these thirty pieces of silver bring us good luck.

FOOL: Good. That's all done, then! I can hardly believe it. I'm so happy. Jesus, hold fast… Salvation is at hand… I'll take the pincers… Here they are… You'd never have thought, would you, Jesus, that a Fool would have come to save you! Ha, ha! Wait a minute while I fasten this belt around you… Don't worry that I'm going to hurt you. I'll bring you down as gently as a bridegroom brings his bride… and then I'll put you over my shoulder, because I'm as strong as an ox, me… And away we go! I'll take you down to the river; there I've got a boat, and with four strokes we'll be across the river. And before day breaks, we'll be safe and sound in the house of a friend of mine, who is a doctor and will give you medicines and cure you within three days. You don't want that? You don't want my sorcerer friend? Alright, then we'll go to the ointment-doctor, who's also a man I know and trust. No? You don't want me to un-nail you?

I see! You think that with these holes in your hands and feet, and with your muscles all torn, the way they've left you, you won't be able to get around any longer, or fend for yourself. You don't want to have to be reliant on others in this world? Am I right? What? It's not even for that reason? It's for the sacrifice? What do you mean, for salvation? For redemption…? What are you talking about…?! What? Oh, poor soul… you're feverish… Look at how you're shivering… Alright, but for the moment I'm taking you down. I'll cover you with this tunic… Now, if you don't mind my saying, you're as stubborn as a mule… You don't want to be rescued? You really want to die on this cross? Yes? For the salvation of man?

Oh, I can't believe it… And they call *me* the Fool, but you beat me by a long chalk, Jesus, my friend! And there I was, breaking my back to win that game of cards, all night, just to have this satisfaction… But by the grail, you are the Son of God, no? That's right, isn't it? I'm not mistaken, am I? Well, then, seeing that you are the Son of God, you know what's going to be the result of you dying here on the cross… I am not God, nor am I a prophet… but the Pale

Lady told me this morning, between her tears, how it's all going to end up.

First of all, they're going to model you all in gold, from head to foot. Then they'll carve your iron nails. All out of silver. Your tears will become sparkling diamonds; and your blood that is now flowing all over the place, they will turn into a stream of shiny rubies. All this they will do to you, you who have shouted yourself hoarse, telling them of poverty. In addition, they'll go putting this pain-bearing cross of yours all over the place: on shields, on banners of war, on swords to kill people as if they were calves, killing in your name, you, who cried aloud that we are all brothers and that we should not kill each other. You've already had one Judas, haven't you? Well, rest assured that the Judases will swarm like ants, betraying you, working to cut your balls off.

Believe me, it's not worth the effort! You don't believe me? So, who's going to be any different? The blessed Francis… and then Nicholas… St Michael Cut-the-cloak… Dominic… Catherine and Clare. Yes, alright, I'll accept that. But these are only a handful, in comparison with the number of rogues… and that handful will end up being treated in just the same way that they've treated you, after they've persecuted them in their lifetime. Say that again… sorry, I didn't catch it. Even if there were only one… Even if there were only one man on the whole earth worthy of being saved, then your sacrifice will not have been in vain… Oh no! Now you really are the chief of all Fools! You're a complete lunatic asylum! The only time I liked you was when you turned up in church and all the traders were there, and you began to beat them all with a big stick. Oh, that was so good to see. *That* should be your job, not dying on the cross for people's salvation! Oh Lord, Lord… I'm going to cry… But I'm crying with anger.

CHIEF CRUCIFIER: Hey, Matazone, you wretch! Haven't you got him down yet? What have you been doing up till now? Sleeping?

FOOL: No, I haven't been sleeping! I've just changed my mind. I don't want to un-nail this Christ after all. It's better that he stays on the cross.

CHIEF CRUCIFIER: Oh, wonderful! And now I suppose you'll want all that gold and silver back... Oh, what a crafty devil! You sent us off to act as porters, to bring this hanged Judas, just so as to make fun of us! Well, no, my dear Matazone. If you want the stuff back, you're going to have to win it back at Tarot! Only on that condition do you get it back!

FOOL: No, I don't want to play. You can keep it all... the money, the gold, the earrings, because I shall never gamble again as long as I live. I won tonight, for the first time, and that's enough for me... Even for just one man who is worthy... it would be worth dying on a cross?! Oh, but you're mad... The Son of God is mad!

Take a stick and beat, beat, all those who trade in church, thieves, swindlers, impostors and rogues. Out with them! Beat them, beat them!

THE PASSION:
MARY AT THE CROSS

WOMAN: See – his mother's coming – the blessed Mary. Run and stop her. Don't let her see him hung up and crucified like a skinned goat, running with blood like a flowing fountain, like a mountain of melted snow in spring, because of the great nails that they've driven into the flesh of his hands and feet, driven right through the bone.

CHORUS: Don't let her see him!

But she will not stop. She runs along the path in despair, and the four of us cannot hold her.

MAN: If four of you cannot hold her, try five, or six... She must not see this son of hers, his body all twisted like the root of an olive tree eaten by ants.

OTHER WOMAN: Hide the Son of God, cover his face, so that his mother doesn't see who he is... We shall tell her that the man on the cross is someone else, a stranger... That it is not her son...

WOMAN: I think that even if we covered the Son of God all over with a white sheet, his mother would still recognise him... It would need only a finger sticking out, or a lock of his hair, because all that was made by her, by his mother.

MAN: She's coming... The blessed Mary has come... It would be more merciful by far to kill her with a knife, rather than let her see her son! Give me a stone. I shall stun her with a blow, so that she falls down and does not see...

OTHER MAN: Be quiet. Move aside... Oh, poor woman, you whom they call blessed... And how can she be blessed with this decoration of four nails that they have hammered and driven into that bleeding flesh, something you would not even do to a poisonous lizard or a bat?

WOMAN: Be quiet! Hold your breath, for now you will hear this woman scream and scream, as if grief had torn her in two, poor wretch; a pain like seven stab wounds, enough to burst her heart asunder.

MAN: Stay there. Don't say a word... At least let her weep a bit. Let her scream! Let her give vent to the pain that is choking her!

OTHER WOMAN: Listen to that silence. Listen to the din of it. There's no point blocking your ears. Say something, say something, Mary... Oh, please!

MARY: Give me a ladder... I want to climb it, to be near to my loved one. My loved one... Oh, my fine, pale, dying son. Don't worry, my beloved, because now your mother is here! What have these murderers, these butchers done to you? These God-forsaken animals? Coming and doing this to my son! What did this big silly boy of mine ever do to you, for you to hate him so much, for you to do such terrible things to him... But I shall make you pay for this, one by one! Oh, you will pay, even if I have to go to the ends of the world to find you. Animals! Beasts! Wretches!

CHRIST: Mother, don't shout, mother.

MARY: Yes, yes. You're right. Forgive me, my dear one, for this outburst and for the angry words I spoke. It was just my grief at finding you here, stained with blood and stripped, kicked, beaten and hung on this cross... with holes in those delicate, fine hands and feet... the feet that I made... the feet that now drip blood, drop by drop... Oh, it must hurt so!

CHRIST: No, mother, don't worry. I promise you, I don't feel pain any more. it has passed. I don't feel anything; go home, mother, go home, please...

MARY: Yes, we'll go home together. I'll come up and bring you down. I'll pull out your nails, gently, gently. Give me a pair of pincers... come and give me a hand... help me, someone!

SOLDIER: Hey, woman, what are you doing up on that ladder? Who gave you permission?

MARY: That's my son that you have crucified... I want to pull his nails out, and take him home with me...

SOLDIER: Home? You're in a hurry! But he's not yet run out his time, holy Virgin, he's not yet well seasoned! Rest assured that the moment he draws his last breath, I'll give a whistle, and you can come and take this young fellow of yours, all packed up and ready to go... Alright? Come down, now...

MARY: No, I'm not coming! I'm not going to leave my son all on his own, to spend the night in this place, dying, all on his own. And you can't do this to me. Because I'm his mother! I am his mother!

SOLDIER: Alright, Mrs Mother-of-him, now I've had enough. Now I'm going to have to bring you down the way we get apples off a tree. Do you want to see how? I give a good shake to this ladder, and you'll come down with a thud, like a big ripe pear.

CHRIST: No! Soldier, as you are a good man, I pray you. Do to me as you will... shake the cross so that it lacerates the flesh of my hands and my bones, but please, I pray you, don't harm my mother...

SOLDIER: Did you hear that, my good lady? And what am I supposed to do now? For me it's all the same: either you come down from that ladder, and fast, or I am going to shake the cross.

MARY: No, no... For pity's sake... wait. I'm coming down. Look, here I am, down already.

SOLDIER: So you finally got the message, woman... And don't look at me with those burning eyes. It's not my fault if that young fellow decides to jump up, spread his arms

and hang there… No, don't think that I don't feel sorry. I know your pain. The glisten of bloody tears that are now falling from your eyes shows the pain and grief of a mother! But I can't do anything to help. I have my orders. This sentence must be carried out. I have been sentenced to make sure that your son dies, or otherwise I'll end up nailed there myself, with those very same nails.

MARY: Oh kind soldier, gentle soldier, take this; I make you a gift of this silver ring… and of these golden earrings… Take them and keep them in exchange for a favour that you can do me.

SOLDIER: What favour is that?

MARY: Let me take water and a rag to clean the blood off my son, and let me give him a bit of water to dampen his lips, all shrivelled with thirst…

SOLDIER: Is that all you want?

MARY: I also ask you to take this shawl and go up on the ladder and put it round his shoulders, under his arms, so as to help him as he hangs there from the cross…

SOLDIER: Oh lady, you do your son a disservice. Do you really want to keep him alive and living, so that he has to suffer all this terrible pain? In your shoes, I would try and help him die as soon as possible!

MARY: Die? Is my sweet one going to have to die, then? His hands, dead, his mouth, dead, and his eyes… and his hair, dead? Oh, they have betrayed me…!

Oh Gabriel, you young man, you with your sweet face, with your voice like a seductive viol, you were the first; you betrayed me like a trickster: you came to tell me that I would be queen… and blessed… happy, blessed among all women! Look at me! Look at me! See how I am reduced. I end up as the last among women!

You knew it, you knew it… When you brought me the 'annunciation', when you moved me with emotion and left me this child flowering in my belly, and I thought that I was going to be Queen of that fine throne! Queen, with a gentle son, a knight, with two spurs, these two great nails, banged into his feet! Why didn't you tell me this before my dream? Oh, you can be sure, I would never have let myself conceive, never, even if God the Father in person had come, instead of this pigeon, this dove, this Holy Ghost, come to wed me…

CHRIST: Mother, has your grief turned you mad, that you blaspheme so? That you say things without knowing what you say? Take her home, brothers, before she collapses with her grief.

MAN: Let us go, Mary. Make your son happy. Leave him in peace.

MARY: No. I shall not! Forgive me… Let me stay here close to him, and I won't say another word against his father. Or against anyone. Leave me… be so kind!

CHRIST: I have to die, mother, and it is hard. I have to let myself go, mother, and use up the breath that keeps me alive… But with you here tormenting your heart, mother, I can't… It just makes it harder…

MARY: I want to help you, my dearest one. Oh, don't make me go! Why can't we both die together, mother and son, so that they can put us, locked into an embrace, into one tomb?

SOLDIER: I told you before, lady! There is only one way to make him happy: kill him at once. If you want to hurry it up and take that lance leaning over there, we soldiers will pretend not to see, and you must run up under the cross and stick the point into him with all your strength, stick the lance right into his belly, right in, and then, in a moment, you will see Christ die. (*The Madonna faints*) What's the matter? Why did she faint? I never even touched her!

MAN: Lay her out… do it gently… and give her room to breathe…

WOMAN: Let's have something to cover her with… she's shivering with the cold…

OTHER MAN: I left my cloak at home…

MAN: Move aside there… Help me to lay her out…

OTHER MAN: And now be quiet and let her recover.

MARY: (*As if in a dream*) Who are you, up there, young man, I seem to know you. What is it that you want from me?

WOMAN: She's talking in her sleep, she's confused… she's having visions…

GABRIEL: I am Gabriel, the Angel of the Lord. I am he, oh Virgin, the herald of your solitary and delicate love.

MARY: Go spread your wings, Gabriel. Return to the radiant joys of Heaven, for there is nothing for you on this vile earth, in this tormented world. Go, so that you do not soil your wings, with their feathers coloured in gentle colours… Don't you see the mud… and the blood… dung and filth…? It's like a sewer… Go, so that your delicate ears are not burst asunder with this desperate crying, the pleading and weeping that arises on all sides. Go, so that you do not sear your bright eyes looking at sores and scabs and boils and flies and worms creeping forth from torn bodies of the dead.

You are not used to this, because in Paradise you have no wailing and lamentation, or wars, or prisons, or men hanged, or women raped. In Paradise there is no hunger, no starvation, nobody sweating with work, wearing themselves to the bone, no children without smiles, no women out of their minds with grief, nobody who suffers to pay the price of original sin. Go, Gabriel, go, Gabriel.

GABRIEL: Grief-stricken woman, whom suffering has struck even in her belly, now I understand clearly… Now that this torment has seized you, seeing the young Lord God nailed up… at this moment, I too understand, just like you…

MARY: You understand, just like me, just like me? Gabriel, did you bear my son in your swelling belly? Did you bite your lip so as not to scream with pain while giving birth to him? Did you feed him? Did you give him the milk from your breast, Gabriel? Did you suffer when he was sick with fever, when he was down with measles, and did you stay up all night comforting him when he was crying with his first teeth? No, Gabriel? Well, if you didn't go through all that, then you cannot speak of sharing my grief at this moment...

GABRIEL: You're right, Mary... Forgive my presumption. I said it because my heart is breaking within me. I, who thought that I was above all suffering. But I come to remind you that it is just this, your song, this lament without a voice, this plaint without sobs, this, your sacrifice, and the sacrifice of your son, which will tear apart the heavens, and which will enable men for the first time to enter Paradise!

APPENDIX

Different cultures might produce different versions of Mistero Buffo. *This edition therefore includes a section from Stuart Hood's own Lallans translation, taken from* The Resurrection of Lazarus.

He's comin. He's comin. He's here.
Wha is he? What ane is he?
Jesus!
What ane?
The wan wi the black face? I dinna like the way he glowers.
No, no. That yin's Mark.
The yin ahint?
The big yin?
No, the wee yin.
The hauflin?
The ane wi the baird ana.
He luiks like a hauflin tae me, dammit if he disna.
Luik! There aa there!
Hey John. I ken him — John. John! Jesus. A real nice face, Jesus.
Luik! there's the Madonna as weel. There's aa his kith and kin. He's aye got them aa wi him.
They dinna let him gae about alane — he's no richt i the heid.
Jesus! Oh I like that yin. He gied me a wink anna!
Jesus, Jesus, dae that miracle wi the laifs and the fishes like that ither time whan they were that guid.
Whaur's the tomb?
Eh? — it's yon ane there.
Oh luik, he's tauld them tae tak aff the muckle stane.

No, I'll nae get down on my knees. I dinna haud wi that.
  That's great.
Wheesht!
Lat me see!
No, get affen that chair!
No, lat me up. I need tae see.
Jesus. Luik. They've taen up the muckle stane. There's the
  deid man, he's in there — it's Lazarus stinkan. Feech!
What's that awfa stink?
Christ!
Whit's wrang?
Wheesht!
Lat me see!
He's fou o wurms — o creepie-crawlies. Feech! He maun
  hae been deid a month — he's a fa'in apairt. That's a fine
  thing they've dun tae him. Tae Jesus. It's nae joke. I fear
  he'll no manage this time, pair thing.
I'm sure he'll no manage it, he canna dae it! There's nae
  wey he cin mak him come oot. He's stinkan rotten.
  That's a fine thing — tellin him he wasna deid mare nor
  three days! It's a month an mair. That's a fine like thing.
  Puir Jesus!
I say he'll manage aa the same, that yin's a haily man at cin
  dae the miracle even if they've been stinkan for a month
  and mair.
And I say he canna.
Will ye wager?
I'll wager anna!
Richt than! Saxpence! A sheelin. Fitever ye like.
I'll haud them. Dae ye trust me? He dis. We aa trust each
  ither. Fine than, I'll tak the money.
Richt than, tak tent though. Doun on yer knees, aabody.
Fit's he daein?
He's there prayin.
Wheesht will ye?
Hey there, Lazarus, git up noo.
Oh, he cin haud forth and he cin sing if he likes — aa at'll
  come oot is the worms he's fou o.
Git up, I bid ye!

Wheesht! he's up on his knees.

Wha? Jesus?

No! Lazarus. God, luik at that.

Get awa wi ye it's nae possible.

Lat me see.

Luik, luik — he's waukin, he's fa'en doon. He's staunan!
On his twa feet.

A meeracle! Oh, it's a meeracle anna. Oh Jesus, ye're a
great ane and I didna believe.

Weel duin, Jesus.

I hae won the wager. Gie's the money. Dinna try ony tricks
wi me!

Weel duin, Jesus.

My purse, they've stawn my purse. Thief!

Weel duin, Jesus.

Thief!

Weel duin, Jesus. Jesus! Weel duin! Thief...